FINDING
FULFILLMENT

A Path to Reclaiming **Hope** and
Empowerment for Educators

Robin Noble

Foreword by Sharon V. Kramer

Copyright © 2020 by Solution Tree Press

Materials appearing here are copyrighted. With one exception, all rights are reserved. Readers may reproduce only those pages marked "Reproducible." Otherwise, no part of this book may be reproduced or transmitted in any form or by any means (electronic, photocopying, recording, or otherwise) without prior written permission of the publisher.

555 North Morton Street
Bloomington, IN 47404
800.733.6786 (toll free) / 812.336.7700
FAX: 812.336.7790

email: info@SolutionTree.com
SolutionTree.com

Visit **go.SolutionTree.com/leadership** to download the free reproducibles in this book.

Printed in the United States of America

Library of Congress Cataloging-in-Publication Data

Names: Noble, Robin, 1963- author.
Title: Finding fulfillment : a path to reclaiming hope and empowerment for educators / Robin Noble.
Description: Bloomington, IN : Solution Tree Press, 2019. | Includes bibliographical references and index.
Identifiers: LCCN 2019023455 (print) | LCCN 2019023456 (ebook) | ISBN 9781947604759 (paperback) | ISBN 9781947604766 (ebook)
Subjects: LCSH: Teacher morale--United States. | Teachers--Job satisfaction--United States. | Teachers--Professional relationships--United States. | Professional learning communities--United States.
Classification: LCC LB2833.2 .N63 2019 (print) | LCC LB2833.2 (ebook) | DDC 371.1001/9--dc23
LC record available at https://lccn.loc.gov/2019023455
LC ebook record available at https://lccn.loc.gov/2019023456

Solution Tree
Jeffrey C. Jones, CEO
Edmund M. Ackerman, President

Solution Tree Press
President and Publisher: Douglas M. Rife
Associate Publisher: Sarah Payne-Mills
Art Director: Rian Anderson
Managing Production Editor: Kendra Slayton
Senior Production Editor: Suzanne Kraszewski
Content Development Specialist: Amy Rubenstein
Copy Editor: Kate St. Ives
Proofreader: Mark Hain
Editorial Assistant: Sarah Ludwig

To the staff of Ramirez Thomas Elementary School (2010–2013): your courage and tenacity in implementing the turnaround model of school reform and the subsequent positive outcomes you facilitated for the students and families of your school community were truly remarkable. I am forever honored and humbled to have been your principal.

Acknowledgments

First, I would like to acknowledge the support and encouragement of Becky DuFour who championed this book from the beginning. Becky graciously read my initial chapters when I was feeling stuck in my writing and questioning whether to move forward. She connected me with Solution Tree Press, ultimately making this book a reality. Becky was a mentor and a huge part of my growth as an educator. I am forever grateful.

Enormous thanks to Douglas Rife and the entire team at Solution Tree Press. It has been an absolute pleasure working with all of you in completing this book. Special thanks to Amy Rubenstein, content development specialist at Solution Tree Press. Your insights, encouragement, and friendship were invaluable during the initial stages of writing this book. Sue Kraszewski, senior production editor, thank you for your help guiding the final touches and nuances in my writing to ensure the message and purpose of this book are clear and accessible to readers. Rian Anderson, many thanks to you and your team for the beautiful cover and text design. And thank you to Kelly Rockhill and the marketing team for your support in making this book visible to many.

Thank you to Jeff Jones for his vision and support of all of us in the Solution Tree family, and thank you to Shannon Ritz and the professional development department for your continued support as we spread a message of hope for schools. I want to acknowledge the PLC associates at Solution Tree who are a continuous source of brilliance, inspiration, and support. I would like to give a particular shout out to Sharon Kramer and all the associates who work so diligently in the priority schools. Your vision and tenacity to ensure *all* students learn at high levels inspires me daily.

Finally, I want to thank my wife, Karolyn Gazella; your willingness to help create the space for my writing, review chapters, and offer unwavering encouragement was invaluable during this process. Your belief in my voice and message and the need to share it has kept me on the path to completing this book. I am so thankful for your love and commitment to my growth as an individual and as an educator. Life is better with you!

Solution Tree Press would like to thank the following reviewers:

Rick Bell
Assistant Principal
New Prague Middle School
New Prague, Minnesota

Andrew Buchheit
Principal
T. Clay Wood Elementary School
Nokesville, Virginia

Dan Draper
Principal
River Grove Elementary School
Lake Oswego, Oregon

Anthony Grazzini
Director of PLCs and Special Projects
Cicero School District #99
Cicero, Illinois

Bryan Hollembeak
Principal
Coronado Elementary
St. Johns, Arizona

Dusti Larsen
Fourth-Grade Teacher
Gravette Upper Elementary
Gravette, Arkansas

Matt J. Navo
Superintendent
Sanger Unified School District
Sanger, California

Kim Timmerman
Principal
Adel DeSoto Minburn Middle School
Adel, Iowa

CJ Waddell
Assistant Principal
Sparks High School
Sparks, Nevada

Table of Contents

Reproducible pages are in italics.

About the Author .... **ix**

Foreword *by Sharon V. Kramer* .... **xi**

Introduction **1**
    A Common Trend 3
    Essential Needs 4
    The Path Forward 7
    Tools for Success 9
    Let's Get Started! 10

1   The Internal Culture of the Educator **11**
    School Culture 12
    The Culture of Public Education 12
    The Internal Culture of the Educator 14
    The Transition From Despondency to Hope 16
    Reflection 20

2   Self-Determination Theory **23**
    Self-Determination Theory 24
    Building a Framework 29
    Reflection 32
    Revisiting Your *Why* 33

3   Autonomy **35**
    Action Research 36
    Tight and Loose Leadership 41
    Reflection 44

4 Competence 45
Recognizing and Addressing a Sense of Incompetence 46
Turning the Tide: Setting Goals for Competence and Increased
    Self-Efficacy 50
Reflective Practice Through Goal Setting 63
Reflection—My SMART Goal 64

5 Relatedness 67
What Relatedness Offers 67
What Is Relatedness? 69
Five Indicators of Team Effectiveness 72
Resilience and the Collaborative Team in a PLC 76
Shared Leadership—Adding Another Lens 86
Reflection 94

6 Finding Your Voice 97
Finding Your Voice and Sharing It 98
First Things First: Letting Go of the Past 101
Autonomous Action Plan 102
Autonomous Action Plan Template *112*

Epilogue 115

References and Resources 119

Index 125

Visit **go.SolutionTree.com/leadership** to
download the free reproducibles in this book.

About the Author

Robin Noble, MEd, is an author, consultant, and presenter with more than thirty years of experience in education. She has served as an elementary school principal, district instructional coach, middle school English teacher, and special education teacher. Most recently, Robin was the principal of a K–5 elementary school servicing a predominantly Mexican-immigrant, English-learner, low-socioeconomic population.

During her tenure as principal, she successfully led the school through the federally funded turnaround model of reform, using the professional learning community (PLC) process as the foundation for the work. The school significantly increased proficiency rates and, after being named the ninth-lowest-performing school in the state just three years earlier, was recognized by the New Mexico Public Education Department as a Top Growth School in 2012. In addition, Robin was recognized with the Award for Student Achievement by the New Mexico School Board Association for her work with her school community and the advancements in student achievement.

Robin specializes in establishing a PLC foundation to usher in influential changes in schools. Her consulting focuses on the importance of creating a culture of high expectations for student learning, developing common language and commitments toward this goal, and facilitating the development of values and systems that lead to effective collaboration, evidence-based learning, and increases in student achievement. Robin also works with educators to help restore a sense of hope and empowerment in their professional lives by developing pathways toward autonomy, competence, and relatedness in the educational setting.

She received her bachelor's degree in education from the University of Central Florida and her master's degree in educational leadership from the University of New Mexico.

To book Robin Noble for professional development, contact pd@SolutionTree.com.

Foreword

by Sharon V. Kramer

Schools and the leaders and educators within them are under intense pressure from all directions, from the local level up to the national. The pressure is especially great in underperforming schools that have declining or stagnant student achievement or have been labeled as failing. In these schools, there is an overwhelming perception that no matter what leaders and teachers do, there is no way out of the downward spiral.

In schools where a cycle of failure permeates the entire system, the emotional and professional pressure educators face can lead to a sense of hopelessness. This combination of pressure and hopelessness is often the reason so many of the best and brightest educators leave the profession.

Viktor Frankl, author of *Man's Search for Meaning* (1959; 2006), writes that the force of human life is that we have made a difference. We want our life to matter. Frankl identifies three fundamental human longings: (1) to be successful (achievement), (2) to belong (connection), and (3) to make a difference (significance). When educators feel hopeless, these fundamental human longings go unfulfilled. Confirmation that what we are doing for students makes a difference in their lives and the world is the fulfillment every educator is seeking. Each of us wants to leave the world a better place because of the work we have done.

In *Finding Fulfillment: A Path to Rediscovering Hope and Empowerment for Educators*, Robin Noble takes the reader on a journey from hopelessness to hopefulness. Robin's work in underperforming schools and districts across North America has helped her craft the authentic, concrete, and practical strategies and tools for overcoming pressure from all directions and finding fulfillment. She brings that experience, expertise, and empathy to this excellent guidebook. Her emphasis on reflection and helping school leaders think critically on the culture of their school or district is a tool she herself uses.

As educators and school and building leaders, we face many stressors that lead to a feeling of hopelessness: negative labels, too many initiatives and programs, top-down mandates in which we have no input, and the all-too-common blame game. As Robin expertly shows, educators must develop a healthy internal culture to combat the feelings of hopelessness these pressures can arouse. In this comprehensive resource, she utilizes the PLC process to forge a how-to pathway for achieving the universal human longings as established by self-determination theory: (1) autonomy, (2) competence, and (3) relatedness.

In this book, Robin raises vital questions such as, "What is fulfillment and how does one find it? What is it that facilitates the development of happiness and well-being? And how can educators find fulfillment and happiness again on a large scale?" (p. 7). In proposing answers, she encourages school leaders to work within their buildings and districts to build a strong, healthy culture by recognizing the three needs of autonomy, competence, and relatedness, using their voices to advocate for them, and empowering teachers and other staff members to do the same. The questions she poses in the reflection section of each chapter might be uncomfortable to consider at times; however, they are amazingly helpful to understand one's own personal journey.

Throughout this book, Robin astutely describes the connections between working as a PLC and finding fulfillment. The PLC process builds and fosters the hope and empowerment necessary for the fulfillment educators seek. The PLC process provides the infrastructure that supports continuous improvement; the way that teachers, teams, and the entire school decide to work together within a PLC on behalf of their students makes discovering or rediscovering fulfillment possible. PLC is an investment in people, not things or programs—it is a way of being (Kramer, 2019).

There is no doubt that the work of educators is significant and important. We all recognize that there would be no doctors, astronauts, engineers, carpenters, electricians, entrepreneurs, writers, or members of any other profession if there were no educators. Educators facilitate the learning that guides entire communities of people throughout their lives. This happens over time, however. Educators often do not realize the fruits of their labor—especially when pressures mount that make it impossible to remember why we joined the profession to begin with. This book helps us all to celebrate our intense, hard work all along the way. It is in these small steps that educators feel true fulfillment and empowerment.

Introduction

Never, however, have America's educators accomplished so much for so many in the face of so many obstacles only to be subjected to unrelenting attacks and condemnation.

—Richard DuFour

In the spring of 2010, I was preparing to address my staff at the Wednesday afternoon staff meeting. We were edging toward the end of what would be my first year as the newly hired principal at a mid-sized K–5 Title I school. Ninety-eight percent of the students qualified for free and reduced lunch. A majority of the school's families had emigrated from Mexico to the United States and 68 percent of the student population identified as learning English as a second language. I was hired the preceding fall after the previous principal had failed to improve student achievement scores over the last several years.

It was the end of the day, and although it occurred every day of the week at 3:15 p.m., the mechanical blare of the dismissal bell was startling. In an instant, the halls were filled with students clamoring toward the exits, mirroring the swarm of thoughts and anxieties swirling in my own mind. You see, I had a message to deliver to my staff that day that would undoubtedly tear the fabric of a school culture that was already hanging by threads.

When I arrived at the library twenty minutes later, teachers and support staff had found their respective places at the tables stationed throughout. They all had what had become a familiar look of end-of-school-day weariness that silently communicated the desire to be anywhere else than a staff meeting. The sound of the HVAC system reverberated above us like a low-flying jet, making it difficult to hear and further lulling the occupants of the room into lethargic melancholy. I, on the other hand, was wired with nervous energy. Unlike the usual nuts and bolts, the message I would deliver on this day would soon change everything . . . for everyone.

Like many public schools in the United States at the time, my school had been identified as one of the lowest-performing schools in the state. Under the leadership of Arnie Duncan and the Obama administration, the U.S. Department of Education had given states a new charge: gather School Improvement Grant (SIG) money supplemented by the American Recovery and Reinvestment Act of 2009 and instead of spreading it out over the growing number of schools in need of improvement, identify your lowest performing schools and funnel it to them. At the end of this process, my school had been ranked the ninth lowest-performing school in our state. The options the district received regarding how to improve our school were: (1) close the school and reallocate students to other better-performing schools; (2) turn the school into a charter school; (3) work through eight identified strategies to bring about increased student achievement while retaining the current staff, otherwise known as the transformational model; or (4) use the same eight strategies as those employed in the transformational model but, in order to receive a clean start on the ladder of school ratings, choose the turnaround model. Both the transformational model and the turnaround model require the principal, if he or she has been the leader for more than two years, to be removed from his or her position. In addition, the turnaround model requires all educators in the school to reinterview for their jobs. The district is then restricted to selecting only 50 percent of the current staff to return the following year (Unites States Department of Education, 2010). It is this final stipulation that makes the turnaround model the most controversial of the four models.

Rumors had swept through the building since our return from winter break, foretelling radical changes. Students had achieved little or no growth on state tests in the previous seven years, and, under No Child Left Behind (NCLB), the school had cascaded through all the various stages of disrepute as a *school in need of improvement*. The school adopted curriculums and programs promising to fix the glaring achievement gap, only to have them end up on dusty bookshelves or as faint memories in the minds of students and teachers alike. It was no wonder the staff was weary. Continued identification as a failing school and a litany of unsuccessful programs had eroded any hope, leaving in its place an underlying fatigue that seemed to stifle any sincere motivation or will to find a way out of the downward spiral.

As I stepped up to the front of the room, I thought about the phone call I had received the night before from the district superintendent. We were getting ready to tread in new, controversial, and uncertain territory. This filled me with a sense of fear and uncertainty that left me tossing in my sleep. Now, standing before my teaching staff, I felt the fear again, even as I gathered my thoughts to deliver what was meant, ultimately, to be a message of hope. I feared that a radical path to hope, the chosen antidote to failure, would wreak havoc not only on this small school, but throughout the district's entire teaching community. I took a deep breath, and as I spoke, I started out on one of the most challenging experiences in my educational career when I told my staff that we would enact reforms using the school turnaround model.

A Common Trend

Although, as the current principal, I was permitted to remain in my position at the school because I had just arrived, at the time I was a relatively new principal and was in no way prepared for the emotional and interpersonal challenges that would follow. Fifty percent of the current teaching staff members were going to lose their jobs at this school. At the outset, teachers were already divided into various camps, and gossip and backbiting would only increase as teachers feared for their positions and, frankly, their careers. Union members and leaders were up in arms, newspaper editorials regarding the process were personal and cutting. One contributor aggressively questioned my abilities to lead a predominantly Spanish-speaking school community as a white, non-Spanish-speaking woman. Just walking into the school each morning during the initial days of the turnaround process was a lesson in how to deal with and address direct hostility. I was the messenger, but I feared that the vision, passion, and determination I had brought with me to begin transforming this low-performing school would be metaphorically killed in the upheaval.

At the time, I thought my school's situation was unique. However, as I started to work with other educators, schools, and districts throughout the United States, I realized that these sudden and dramatic repositionings of principals and educators happen more often than one might think. The emotional and professional damage that educators experience when they have no control is also more prevalent than one might think, and this damage can leave scars.

Essential Needs

I started writing this book to address the experience of powerlessness I was seeing in educators before it causes irreversible damage and leaves scars that are difficult to erase. I saw how widespread ineffectual and demeaning trends are in schools throughout North America and the negative impact these trends have on educators. Labeling is one such trend. It can hurt an educator's sense of worth and self-respect. You will likely recognize certain damaging labels from your own work as an educator—labels like *In Need of Improvement*, *Restructuring*, *Low-Performing*, *Corrective Action*, or worse yet, *Failing*. The labels cause educators who work in labeled schools to feel anxiety, shame, and a sense of isolation within the professional arena. Then, adding insult to injury, the local news publishes these labels, delivering yet another level of unnecessary shame and pain.

Another ineffective and damaging trend schools and educators face is an onslaught of mandated programs and curriculums that claim to be the *silver bullet* to improve achievement. Yet when these initiatives fail to produce the expected results, policymakers don't ask why they failed, and then validate what is or is not working. Instead, too often the teachers or administrators take the blame while policymakers move on to the next initiative that they think is sure to increase student achievement. This has led to lengthy teacher evaluations that take hours of the administrator's time, increasingly rely on student proficiency rates as a measure, yet produce very little impact on student achievement (Dynarski, 2016).

Although both destructive labeling of schools and lack of meaningful investigation by policymakers into the reasons for an initiative's failure are unsettling, the most disturbing trend I've witnessed in my work in schools is that educators are increasingly removed from the collective inquiry and decision-making processes that go into deciding the best actions needed to help their students achieve. Instead of providing educators with the time and support to be actively involved in researching and deciding what systems, processes, pedagogy, and structural changes need to be implemented, policymakers and employees of the state and district often decide—with little or no input from the educators in the schools themselves—upon an array of curriculums, programs, assessments, and reform proposals that teachers must master and implement with fidelity. Even more maddening, these implementations are too often mandated by decision makers who are completely removed from the educators and the students they serve. Research reminds us that when any group of individuals, including educators, loses the ability to define and solve the problems they face, they also lose the drive, motivation, and sense of self-efficacy that keep them moving forward toward their goals (Margolis & McCabe, 2006; Pink, 2009). So, should it be any surprise to us that our school reform efforts are failing students? Or that educators are leaving the profession in unprecedented numbers?

I realized that educators are not just burned out, they are demoralized and despondent. It isn't that they don't care deeply about their students or don't want to do what is best for them; rather, they experience an underlying current of doubt that the situation will ever actually change, that the next initiative will actually stick, or that they will have the ability and autonomy to impact that change through their expertise and influence. Educators often feel their voices have been silenced and their opinions negated. What has become clear, as I talk with educators throughout the United States and beyond, is an unmistakable and imminent need for educators to find a renewed sense of well-being, fulfillment, and, dare I say happiness in their professions.

I started asking myself some questions. What is fulfillment and how does one find it? What is it that facilitates the development of happiness and well-being? And how can educators find fulfillment and happiness again on a large scale? As it turns out, our popular culture is obsessed with the idea of how to find happiness and fulfillment, so there is a lot of relevant information out there. As I looked at the research through the lens of the educator in the school, a path began to emerge through the plethora of ideas and information—a path that connects happiness and fulfillment to the personal power that stems from the autonomy to make choices, the competence that comes from fulfilling those choices, and from a meaningful role within a social context that is maintained and reinforced by positive relationships with others. With regard to our work as professionals in our schools and districts, these three essential ingredients are effectively defined through Self-Determination Theory (Ryan & Deci, 2000). These three are as follows.

1. The need for autonomy in meeting our goals.
2. The need to feel competent in meeting those goals.
3. The need to feel a sense of relatedness to others as we work toward attaining our goals.

The research definitively points to and supports these essential needs, but they also just make sense intuitively. Because of this, although they have too often been removed from or ignored in the culture of public education, their intuitive relevance jumpstarts our work back to actively meeting these essential needs.

Another realization I came to, as I began to delve into the human need for autonomy, competence, and relatedness, is that the principles of the Professional Learning Communities at Work (PLC) process (DuFour, DuFour, Eaker, Many, & Mattos, 2016) support the educator in developing all three of these critical needs. In *Learning by Doing*, Richard DuFour, Rebecca DuFour, Robert Eaker, Tom Many, and Mike Mattos (2016) define a PLC as "an ongoing process in which educators work collaboratively in recurring cycles of collective inquiry and action research to achieve better results for the students they serve" (p. 10). More specifically, the foundational three big ideas of a PLC—(1) a focus on student learning, (2) a collaborative culture with collective responsibility, and (3) a focus on results—correlate directly with our need for autonomy, competence, and relatedness. I watched these three big ideas transform the school culture and community of my own school as we began to implement the turnaround model. We used the PLC model of shared leadership, action research, and collective responsibility to determine our focus and initiatives. We used data to fine tune our practices that ultimately brought about increases in student achievement that fostered our sense of competence in meeting our goals. We developed a culture of relational trust that allowed us to successfully collaborate and support one another in achieving success for ourselves and for our students.

I can validate how PLCs support the three basic needs of autonomy, competence, and relatedness through my own personal experience. However, I can also bear witness through the stories, personal victories, and documented successes of other educators I've worked with across the United States. In fact, you can find examples of schools across the globe who are on the journey to PLC transformation and have seen how the process, with its focus on learning, collaboration, and results, has improved the achievement of students in their schools and districts while also improving the function and well-being of the educators. (Visit www.allthingsplc.info/evidence to access research and stories from schools and districts that have successfully transformed into PLCs.)

The Path Forward

This book focuses on charting a path forward through meeting the three critical human needs of educators. I set this path forward within the framework of the PLC process. As we embark on a journey through each of these basic human needs, I will give you the tools to restore your sense of empowerment and self-efficacy through conscious attention to these basic needs. I will clearly delineate how implementing the PLC model of cultural and structural reform provides verifiable answers for meeting these three critical needs and restoring your belief in your ability to effect change in your schools and districts. The intended outcome is to guide you on a path back to your true calling and passion for your work as an educator. Personal drive and passion provide the motivation and urgency to keep you in the arena of school reform with a belief that all students can learn at high levels. While this book focuses on the educators and principals in K–12 schools throughout North America, it is relevant and critical to all who provide support and leadership to those schools at the state and district level as well.

In chapter 1, I identify three cultures in public education: (1) the school culture, (2) the culture of public education, and (3) the internal culture of the educator. Although all are important, I focus primarily on what I have come to call the *internal culture of the educator*. In the current climate in public education, many educators have lost the belief that they can actually impact change (MetLife Inc., 2013; *Phi Delta Kappan*, 2019). In order to create systemic changes, healing the internal culture of the educator must come first. Our goal will be to discover (or rediscover) the mindsets and actions that will lead you to once again thrive in your profession—to restore that part of you that believes in your own power and expertise to improve learning for all students and transform the way we do education.

Chapter 2 further examines the research behind well-being and fulfillment. The focus will be on the three innate needs identified in Self-Determination Theory (SDT): autonomy, competence, and relatedness (Ryan & Deci, 2000). These three innate needs are identified as critical to finding fulfillment and well-being in life and in the education profession. In this chapter, I also explore how the PLC processes support the fulfillment of these innate needs in your school or district. I will do this by asking you to revisit times in your life and careers when these needs were fulfilled and review their impact on your sense of self-efficacy and value. And finally, you will revisit the reasons you entered education in the first place. It is imperative to clarify these reasons, so you can secure a solid foundation from which to develop your personal action steps to ensure autonomy, competence, and relatedness going forward.

Chapters 3, 4, and 5 examine the actions and circumstances that you as an educator can identify, support, and act on to reinforce and enhance autonomy, competence, and relatedness. Chapter 3 looks more closely at why autonomy is so critical for the educator. You will also discover ways to bring autonomous action into your day-to-day work in the classroom to support this important innate need, *even* if you are working within larger frameworks that dictate to some extent what goals you set in your work. Chapter 4 identifies how taking focused action that moves us out of our comfort zones and challenges the status quo is the first step in building a strong sense of competency. Through focused goal setting and celebrations of your accomplishments, you will learn how to secure your need for competence while simultaneously supporting autonomy and relatedness. Finally, in chapter 5, I delve into the need for relatedness and how working and collaborating closely with colleagues allow us to attain collective goals, build relational trust, and ultimately meet our needs for relatedness.

In chapter 6, I will ask you to consider ways to find your voice. Too often, educators fall into a victim mentality and blame the system for their discontent. As you work through the steps of fortifying your need for autonomy, competence, and relatedness, your internal culture as an educator will also begin to heal and you will begin feeling a renewed sense of empowerment. With this new sense of well-being and empowerment, it will be important to consider how you can begin influencing educational practice from the bottom up instead of waiting for someone at the top to swoop in and be the rescuer. You will begin to identify ways you can share your expertise and understanding, to demonstrate how education can move to a new paradigm of improving outcomes for educators and students that begins with you.

This book is not about placing blame on yourself for things outside your influence or control. Its purpose is to take back your power as an educator, especially for those who have started to ask the question, "What if I can't do this anymore?"

I was part of a reform process that stemmed from top-down decision making. The school turnaround model came from a federal reform initiative, and then from a district level decision-making process. Nonetheless, educators at my school did hard work as a community and as individuals to move out of any sense of being victimized by the system. We learned that autonomy, competence, and relatedness are not given to us by others; we claim them with our own visions and determination. They reside in the reflective practices of educators, their courageous actions, and their common commitments to their students and communities. It is through this vision and the empowering actions you take that you will ensure that you can respond to the question, "What if I can't do this anymore?" with a resounding, "Yes, I can! And I will!"

Tools for Success

In this book, I will introduce tools to help you state and organize your priorities, solidify personal and professional goals, and identify the actions you intend to take to reclaim your power and influence in your vocation as an educator. Throughout this book, I will ask you to write reflectively on your own experiences in education that have challenged your belief in the system and on your sense of yourself as an educator. I have used reflective writing extensively in both my professional and personal practice for many years. Research shows that reflective writing helps aid both the process of identifying and framing difficult life experiences and moving through them to find hope at the other end (Pennebaker, 2004). The phrase *difficult life experiences* may seem a little out of character for a book directed toward the educator. However, as educators, we have experienced things in our profession that qualify as difficult life experiences.

Psychologist James Pennebaker of the University of Texas at Austin is one of the foremost authorities on reflective writing. Pennebaker has studied the power of writing about life experiences to lift negative mindsets for several decades (Pennebaker, 1991, 1997, 2004; Pennebaker & Smyth, 2016). In his studies, he puts together two separate groups of individuals who have recently been through a challenging life event. In one of the groups, he asks participants to write about the emotionally significant event. He continually finds that the individuals in the groups that write about their thoughts and emotions about the event have statistically significant improvement in physical and mental well-being (Pennebaker, 2004).

When I ask you to reflect at different times throughout this book, I use questions and prompts to encourage you to write on challenging experiences you've encountered in your career as an educator, and on those things you want to act on and change. Holding and honoring your journey, your thoughts, feelings, and intentions, are important pieces of our work together. The research tells us reflective writing aids the necessary process of healing and moving forward, and this is our most important goal (Pennebaker, 1991, 1997, 2004; Pennebaker & Smyth, 2016).

Another caveat of Pennebaker's (2004) work is that those groups that showed significant gains in mental and physical well-being did not simply vent about their experiences and hold on to resentments. They instead used the writing experience to let go, disengage, reframe, and move forward from their disappointments or challenges. I encourage you to do this as well. Moving forward and letting go of negative feelings allows you to retain the energy to make meaningful changes.

With this in mind, I ask you to keep something to write in as you work through this book: a laptop, a tablet, a journal, whatever feels most comfortable to you. If writing is not your thing, then find another vehicle to chart your thinking and goals moving forward. Whatever you choose, please keep it close at hand. We will use it frequently.

Let's Get Started!

Let me say at the outset, it is my honor to be taking this journey with you. If we are truly going to impact the lives of *all* students, ensuring each student has access to every opportunity to pursue the life of his or her choosing, the answers to inspiring their successful education lie within the educators in the schools and classroom. Making this intention a reality will require your commitment to confront difficult truths, change attitudes, and find the inner strength to develop the processes, systems, and best practices that not only impact your students' growth, but impact your growth as an educator and change maker. The journey of reconciliation and healing is a must, but with it comes a way forward and the vision for a new future in your career as an educator.

1

The Internal Culture of the Educator

If you are a public school educator in the United States, you have likely heard a great deal about the importance and impact of school culture in bringing about high academic achievement for all students. Yet two other cultures of equal importance are rarely spoken about: (1) the culture of public education and (2) the internal culture of the educator, both of which I speak about in the introduction. All three of these cultures are crucial and intricately linked. The health of one has the potential to dictate the health of the others. I focus on acknowledging and restoring the internal culture of the educator. This internal culture probably is not talked about on your school's personal development days or found on the agenda of your district in-service days. However, it is critical to restoring hope and empowerment to educators.

Before we explore the internal culture of the educator in the school setting, we must establish a working understanding of what we mean by *school culture*, *the culture of public education*, and *the internal culture of the educator*. These definitions will provide a foundation and common vocabulary as we begin our journey together.

> *Substantial cultural change must precede structural change, for while technical changes are necessary to improve our schools, they produce few positive results when the people using them do not believe in the intended outcome of the change.*
>
> —Anthony Muhammad

School Culture

I begin with school culture because it is of huge importance and impact as we look at school reform and closing the achievement gap. I also use it as the foundation for defining the culture of public education. In his book *Transforming School Culture: How to Overcome Staff Division*, Anthony Muhammad (2018) clearly and convincingly identifies the subversive nature and dangers of unchecked divisive rhetoric, unchallenged belief systems, and toxic norms in a school. If you are an educator who has had the privilege of working in a school or district with a positive culture, you know the value it has not only for the students, but also for the educators. Educators in these schools exist within a community where all members believe in the ability of all students to learn at high levels. The value of working collectively to meet this goal is recognized as key to improved achievement for all, and the educators who make up those teams are honored for their insights and accomplishments. Not only do they share a firm belief that all students can and will learn at high levels, they believe they are the ones to collectively do whatever it takes to achieve this goal.

Muhammad (2018) uses Kent D. Peterson's work on school culture (Cromwell, 2002) to give foundation to his definition of a healthy school culture, and I cite it here to frame our conversation.

> Educators have an unwavering belief in the ability of all their students to achieve success, and they pass that belief on to others in overt and covert ways. Educators create policies and procedures and adopt practices that support their belief in every student's ability. (Muhammad, 2018, p. 20)

I love this definition. It's simple, focused, and effectively captures what we know to be necessary to break through achievement gaps and limited expectations in our schools.

The Culture of Public Education

We can use the preceding definition of a healthy school culture to flesh out a working definition of a healthy culture of public education. What if politicians, policymakers, boards, and superintendents at the federal, state, and local school levels adopted a similar definition of a healthy culture of public education? It might read like the following.

> **Educational policymakers, board members, and leaders at the federal, state, and local levels** have an unwavering belief in the ability of all their **educators** to achieve success, and they pass that belief on to others in overt or covert ways and they create policies and procedures that support their belief in the **ability of every educator**.

That's a definition that if followed could have powerful impact, isn't it? Unfortunately, this type of culture is scarce in the hierarchy of public education. Instead of an "unwavering belief" in educators, education has been infiltrated by policies that would suggest just the opposite, such as the marketing and implementation of *teacher-proof* textbooks, programs, and assessment protocols. In his book *Addicted to Reform: A 12-Step Program to Rescue Public Education*, John Merrow (2017) sums up the idea of teacher-proofing and how it secured a foothold in the culture of public education. He states, "Because [NCLB] school reform demands that students pass tests, we tell teachers how to teach, with scripted curricula that tell them what to say and when. Teachers are robbed of autonomy but held accountable for results" (p. 65). In addition, we have seen the onset of punitive accountability measures that clog the schedules and eat up the time of principals and teachers to do the appropriate work that has been proven to impact student learning and achievement. Instead of showing confidence in educators, such policies leave the educator marginalized and powerless, in both overt and covert ways, in the face of increasing mandates. Merrow (2017) concludes his reflection on these often demoralizing policies by stating, "And we wonder why so many excellent teachers cannot wait to get out [of public education]!" (p. 65). There is definitely truth found in this statement.

The culture of public education clearly plays a large part in the despondency educators face in their profession now. It cannot be overlooked, and it certainly needs to change. But it will change only if the voices of the educators in schools and districts become strong and clear. This is why the healing and restoration of the internal culture of the educator is so important.

The Internal Culture of the Educator

Now that we've explored definitions and aspects of the school culture and the culture of public education, let's define the internal culture of the educator. Studies show that certain qualities and attitudes—for instance, optimism, creativity, resilience, hardiness, and confidence—make an individual more likely to achieve at high levels and attain the goals he or she has set for him- or herself (Duckworth, 2016; Zolli & Healy, 2013). Collectively, these qualities are often referred to as *grit* and relate to one's perseverance in completing a difficult task (Duckworth, 2016). Research has also characterized what is known as a *growth mindset*, a belief that our intelligence and capabilities are not fixed but can be built upon, nurtured, and expanded, thus providing the motivation and determination for continual growth and improvement (Dweck, 2007). These researchers build upon another body of research into what motivates one to stay the course and complete the task set before him or her. This block of research focuses on self-efficacy, a concept pioneered by Harvard professor Albert Bandura and his colleagues. Bandura (1994) defines *self-efficacy* as "a person's beliefs about their capabilities to produce designated levels of performance that exercise influence over events that affect their lives" (p. 1).

It turns out that our thoughts and subsequent beliefs about our abilities to accomplish a task impact the ability to stick with a challenging goal and accomplish it. To more clearly define the internal culture of the educator, I reword Bandura's definition of self-efficacy so it speaks directly to the educator:

> The internal culture of the educator is the internal perceptions and self-talk of the educator that dictate their belief about their capabilities to accomplish the task of ensuring all students learn at high levels.

I have already examined trends in current school policies that potentially erode educators' beliefs that they can successfully ensure high levels of learning for all students. However, I want to make an important distinction here. When I talk about educators' beliefs in their abilities to be successful, I'm not necessarily talking about their skills or abilities as educators; rather, I'm talking about how educators *feel* about their potential to make a positive impact on students. Educational policies often block the educator from feeling like he or she can make that impact. Such policy obstacles can come in many forms; however, I would like to look at two in particular. First, far too often, educators are told to *comply* and *follow* instead of research, discover, contribute, adapt, and lead. Instead of feeling as though they can exercise influence in their schools and classrooms to impact their students' achievement, teachers and principals too often find their opinions suppressed, derailed, or ignored. Second, educational policies and processes can actually oppress educators to such an extent that they simply decide that they just can't do it anymore. Educators' ability to nurture self-efficacy is derailed when the policies and practices of the educational system are continually discouraging. The internal culture of the educator is weakened instead of nurtured, and the outcomes can be demoralizing to the individual and ultimately negatively impact the culture of the school and public education at large.

Let me relay a story about a teacher in a school that had been labeled "low performing," even though she had just finished helping her school turn that trend of low performance around. In three years' time, Evelyn and her grade-level team made a huge impact on the academic performance of students in their classes. Evelyn taught a sixth-grade bilingual classroom in a school that served a majority of English learners, and in which all students came from families living in poverty. This school had been trending in failure for several years, and as a result, many students had been two or three grade levels behind for years. Nonetheless, Evelyn and her team managed to increase proficiency rates in the sixth grade by almost 30 percent in both reading and mathematics.

Unfortunately, Evelyn and her school community had little time to celebrate these successes before the ominous cloud of teacher accountability hit their state. The following year, teachers would be evaluated based on student achievement scores on the state test. For those working in low-performing schools, being compared to teachers in other schools—or being compared to other teachers based on a state test at all—was an unnerving position to be in. For Evelyn, even though her students' scores had increased significantly over the last three years, the idea of being judged and the fear of falling short was too much. When Evelyn showed up at her principal's office at the end of the year, the principal was shocked when she told him she had chosen to leave the profession and would not be back in the classroom next year. Although he tried to persuade this young teacher to stay, her mind was made up. Between family responsibilities and the added pressure of knowing she would be critically evaluated by a standardized test that was being created in the throes of the move to Common Core State Standards, she couldn't manage the pressure. She didn't believe she could do it. So instead of continuing in her position of proven impact on student achievement, she left the profession. As an educator, she felt her value and relevance had been ignored and disregarded for too long. She no longer believed she could do it under these circumstances.

There are two takeaways from this story that I want to emphasize. One is the example it represents of how the culture of public education continues to enact legislation that can very easily be interpreted as, "I don't believe in you," which in turn can erode the motivation and confidence of the educator. And two, it illustrates the common internal thought processes of educators that are not always evident to observers. Vulnerability can be difficult for all of us. Most of us don't like to admit we're overwhelmed or can't do something. It's a hard place to be, particularly if it's in the context of our vocations. And, if you happen to find yourself in a school culture that does not value collaboration and collective responsibility, it can be extremely isolating and exhausting. Even if you have colleagues you feel you can confide in, if no strong culture of relational trust focused on the right work of educators is present, these discussions often happen behind closed doors, become negative in nature, and feed teachers' fears and insecurities, causing the silent erosion of confidence and self-efficacy. This example shows us in a very concrete way how subtle, negative thoughts and beliefs of teachers about their abilities to be effective educators under the given circumstances can begin to erode the will of even the most celebrated, high-achieving educators. And because it is often hidden in the negative self-talk or thoughts of the educator, it may not surface until it is too late. When educators continue to work in school environments that cause them to doubt their worth, this doubt can potentially pull at the strings that unravel the school culture as well.

The Transition From Despondency to Hope

A story like Evelyn's is hard to hear. What can happen to one has the potential to happen to any of us, and we are protective of one another as fellow educators. However, in the pages of this book, we are navigating a different path, one that leads away from feelings of hopelessness and toward empowerment and confidence in our abilities to effect change. We focus on the internal culture of the educator for this very reason. Most experts agree that the outcomes of mandates related to the No Child Left Behind and Race to the Top initiatives have left in their wake many educators who struggle with feelings of hopelessness and powerlessness that have undoubtedly stifled forward progress in truly transforming schools and ushering in better outcomes for everyone in the school community. One can't ignore that this long-term trend of taking away from educators the decision-making power and ability to innovate can lead to feelings of victimization—never a good place to be and certainly not a place to stay. Muhammad (2015) has researched how mindsets impact the educator. He speaks about the victim mindset and notes that those who fall into this mindset find comfort in "framing others as predators and oneself as a victim" (Muhammad, 2015b). Muhammad further states that this mindset feeds the status quo when what education desperately needs is change. This resonated with me. Why? Because change is hard and fear of this change can lead to isolation and a tendency to simply do things the way they've always been done. The fear of this change fits perfectly into the victim mindset where, as Muhammad (2015a) points out, the following three characteristics prevail:

1. Irresponsibility: I'm not responsible for what is happening. In fact, I'm powerless. Therefore, I have a right to be complacent.

2. Low motivation: How can I be responsible for motivation when it is taken from me by others? No one rewards me or appreciates me.

3. Low expectations: What can you expect under these conditions? I'm just trying to keep my head above water.

These attitudes stifle growth and, if not addressed, ensure that the very things that have stolen our initiative will continue to dominate the landscape of public education. Again, this is not where you want to land; however, a lack of self-efficacy and an ongoing internal belief that one is powerless to effect change create a toxic internal culture. These mindsets represent the flawed ways in which educators have come to view and respond to education policies and systems that disregard the educator's knowledge and expertise. Figure 1.1 (page 18) illustrates how this looks viewed through a lens that encompasses the progressive impact of cultures of education. The disempowering nature of public educational policy slowly infiltrates the district culture, the school culture, and finally (or simultaneously), the internal culture of the educator. The story of Evelyn illustrates how this happens in schools and districts. A policy sent down from federal and state agencies that requires districts to compare teachers based on test scores and reward some with merit pay while leaving others unrecognized or punished can set up a culture of unhealthy competition and distrust that impacts not only the internal culture of the educator but the school culture as well. I've watched teachers in a merit-pay system start to resent having to take a student identified as needing special education services or English language learners in their classrooms as they feel it will impact their classroom results on state test averages. I've watched in astonishment as a corporate model of competition that is touted to bring about higher levels of student achievement in schools actually does the opposite by destroying the school culture of collective responsibility and relational trust.

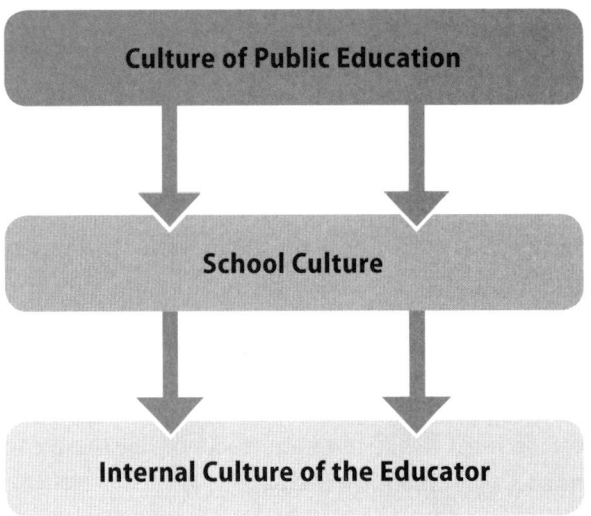

FIGURE 1.1: Top-down culture of influence.

However, here is the good news: mindsets can be changed. Changing them is partly a matter of starting to recognize when you begin to go down the slippery slope of frustration and negativity in your thoughts and actions. We must pay attention when the indicators of gossip or resignation and apathy become apparent—without judgment. If you're saying to yourself, "Wow, that's me! How did this happen?" I can assure you, you're not alone. It happens to the best of us. However, if you continue in this thought pattern, a victim mindset takes hold. And as stated before, this is not where we're going to land. How your internal perceptions and self-talk affect how you feel about yourself and your abilities is widely researched in psychology (Morin, 2016; Neck & Manz, 1992). Educators' internal self-talk can become particularly negative when they feel frightened, overwhelmed, and unable to control or alter the factors causing these feelings. Considering the extraneous (at best) and punitive (at worst) nature of some of the feedback educators receive, you might expect that over time, they develop an increasing lack of confidence and self-efficacy. Just like your students, if you are uninvolved in the *why* of what you are doing or lack the ability to set and celebrate attainable goals on the path to the collective vision and commitments, then it's very difficult to nurture your confidence and self-efficacy.

I ask you to consider flipping the dynamic represented in figure 1.1. If educators want to reimagine schools and districts, take back professionalism, and impact student learning, the change must happen with you and the collective commitments you create with your colleagues in your school, department, or district (see figure 1.2). You must be able to show that your collective efforts, both internal by changing your mindsets and external through the actions you take in your educational settings, are the catalyst for the positive changes you seek. Both internal and external changes hold the answers to the achievement outcomes you long to create for your students. No longer the victim—instead, the crusader!

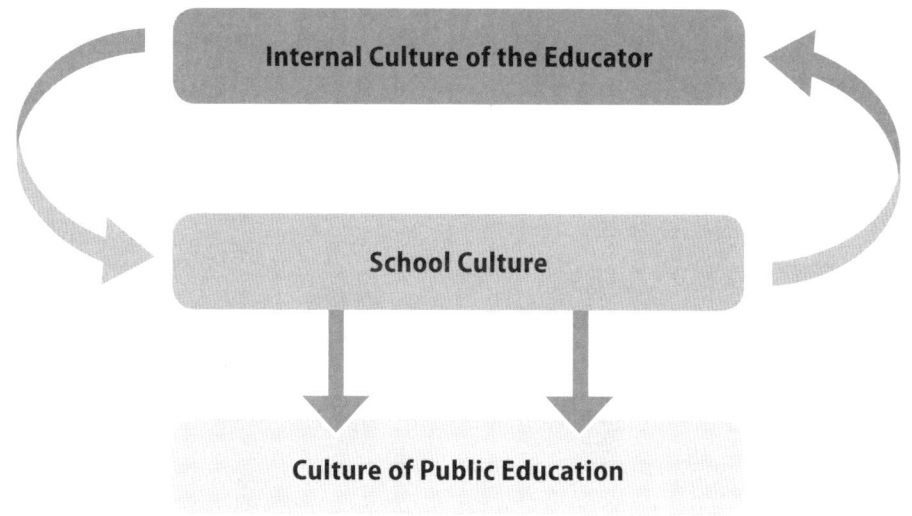

FIGURE 1.2: Internal culture of influence.

This new dynamic stipulates that educators can no longer sit back and blame things outside of their control for lack of student engagement and achievement. While there will always be factors outside our control that affect the things we do, committing to the new dynamic allows us to increase our internal locus of control and thus effect positive changes we may not have believed we were capable of. The new mindset allows us to make inroads into changing the top-down dynamic into a bottom-up dynamic, one that starts and ends where it all matters—with the day-to-day experiences of learning. You must become warriors for yourselves and for your students to ensure high levels of learning for all. However, to be warriors, you must believe first in your mission and then in your power to complete that mission. There is a level of courage needed; putting aside thoughts of frustration and finding a more positive mindset will be necessary. This is where the PLC processes come in.

The PLC process is a highly researched model of transforming the way educators work together collaboratively to ensure learning for all students, and is an incubator for the healing and change that educators are looking for. It is this healing and change that will restore the internal culture of the educator. As our conversations delve into autonomy, competence, and relatedness and their importance in bringing a sense of fulfillment and well-being, you will begin to see how the PLC processes support and bolster your beliefs about your abilities to not only increase student learning, but ultimately, the culture of public education as well.

In the following chapters, we look more closely at autonomy, competence, and relatedness as vehicles to restore the internal culture and at how the PLC process supports our work together. But before we move on, let's do some reflective writing.

Reflection

I would like to introduce our first reflective writing exercise. We've explored some of the challenges and inequities that educators face in the educational system and at this point there may be some thoughts or feelings that have come to the surface. So, I invite you now to get out the reflection tool of your choice (a journal, laptop, and so on) and get started. As you answer the reflective questions I've identified for you, I want you to put it all out there. Don't hold back! And remember to take your time with this. Think about each question. And, as I mentioned in the previous chapter, write down your thoughts and express them in whatever way works for you. All of them. Go ahead and take as little or as much time as you need to respond to the following three prompts.

1. Has there been a time in your career as a professional educator when you felt powerless? If so, what school did you teach or lead in? What grade level did you work with? What district did you support?

2. What happened that made you feel powerless? Was it a district initiative, a state policy, a federal mandate? Was it an unsupportive culture in your school where you felt isolated? Maybe you felt your voice and input were not valued. Whatever the situation, take time to think about the details of this experience and write them down.

3. Why did you feel powerless? How were you limited?

Now, I'd like you to take some time to go back and read over what you wrote. Try to get in touch with what you were, or are, thinking and feeling. Like most people when they go through a demoralizing or fearful situation, your first instincts are probably to either fight or retreat. The fight-or-flight response is embedded deep in all of us. If you're a fighter, you probably became angry. Maybe you railed at the system. Or perhaps you found someone or something to blame. If you're a person who tends to retreat from stress or conflict, perhaps you isolated yourself. Maybe you said to yourself, "This is crazy! I can't believe this is happening! What more can they throw at me or expect of me? What if things never change?" A common response is to decide, "I'm just going to close my door and survive." Regardless of whether your tendency is toward fight or flight, or a little of both, the impact of feeling victimized is real. And, yes—I want you to get in touch with it.

Before I move on, I ask you to answer one more question. Where are you now on this journey of trying to reconcile a profession that can sometimes seem to disrespect you? Which of the characteristics described by Muhammad (2015a)—irresponsibility, low motivation, and low expectations—describes a road you've been down, or one you are currently traveling? Have you felt angry, tired, defeated, or hopeless in the past or in your current situation? Or is your current situation improving? Perhaps you have a new principal, or a new vision and mission for your school. Maybe you're excited that you will have some autonomy in piloting programs and interventions for your school—but you still carry with you some lingering negative mindsets. Wherever you've landed at this point, reflect on where you are now.

After you complete this exercise, I'm going to ask you to set aside those thoughts and reflections that expose your frustration and pessimism. Yes, all the justified anger, all the bitter thoughts, and all the resentments. Or if you've landed at apathy, I ask you to let that go as well. At this stage of the game, all of these defense responses have a very real potential to turn on you and become self-doubts instead of the justified anger you think they represent. So, as best you can, leave it all there on the page for right now—all of it. We'll come back to it later, but for now, we'll focus instead on a new vision for you and your school, and the incredible potential you have to impact the very educational system you may feel has betrayed you. Our goal is to renew your confidence in yourself as an educator and your impact on the students you teach and serve and the system of public education.

2
Self-Determination Theory

When I first began researching these three innate human needs—autonomy, competence, and relatedness—and their importance in maintaining a sense of happiness and well-being, I found myself thinking, "This is obvious, of course we need these in our lives!" They resonated, even if I did not immediately recognize their importance as a critical piece of feeling fulfilled.

Deci & Ryan's research on Self-Determination Theory highlights the potential that nurturing and supporting educators toward meeting these three needs offers for restoring the internal culture of the educator. When educators' need for autonomy, competence, and relatedness is nurtured, such support creates a sense of excitement and motivation, along with a deep sense of ownership and perseverance to meet their intended goals. At times in my own career when each of these needs were met, they fed my sense of self-efficacy and confidence as I completed tasks and fulfilled commitments. But when these needs are thwarted, my own experiences also show that the opposite feelings develop. I'm going to share some of those reflections, but first I'll more clearly define the aspects of Self-Determination Theory.

Conditions supporting the individual's experience of autonomy, competence, and relatedness are argued to foster the most volitional and high-quality forms of motivation and engagement for [action], including enhanced performance, persistence, and creativity.

—Center for Self-Determination Theory

Self-Determination Theory

Self-Determination Theory (SDT) developed out of the ongoing research of psychologists Edward Deci and Richard Ryan from the University of Rochester. Deci and Ryan have been researching the impact of autonomy, competence, and relatedness since 1985, and their work continues to be supported by numerous studies conducted by international scholars across the globe, many of whom contribute to Deci and Ryan's Center for Self-Determination Theory website (selfdeterminationtheory.org). A close look at the research indicates these three innate needs span cultures, countries, and professions. SDT is defined as a *meta-theory*, a critical exploration of a theory that has arisen from research in a particular field of study, that focuses on:

> How social and cultural factors facilitate or undermine people's sense of volition and initiative, in addition to their well-being and the quality of their performance. Conditions supporting the individual's experience of autonomy, competence, and relatedness are argued to foster the most volitional and high-quality forms of motivation and engagement for activities, including enhanced performance, persistence, and creativity. In addition, SDT proposes that the degree to which any of these three psychological needs is unsupported or thwarted within a social context will have a robust detrimental impact on wellness in that setting. (Center for Self-Determination Theory, n.d.)

This description contains a pretty powerful assertion. Over thirty years of research with consistent findings continues to support the importance of autonomy, competence, and relatedness. These three factors not only foster a sense of happiness and fulfillment, they also provide intrinsic motivation to meet one's set goals with perseverance and creativity. So let's clarify these three innate needs as they are defined in the research.

- *Autonomy* is "the integrity, volition and vitality that accompanies self-regulated action" (Deci & Ryan, 2000, p. 254). In other words, it is the innate need to be engaged and in control of determining the actions to take in solving and accomplishing the tasks put before us; we feel empowered.

- *Competence*, simply stated, is "the pleasure [derived] from being effective" (Deci & Ryan, 2000, p. 253). It represents the need to carry out an action and learn that the results of our actions can bring about positive outcomes. We feel effective and thus foster self-efficacy.
- *Relatedness* is the universal need to "cohere with one's group, to feel connection and caring, to internalize group needs and values in order to coordinate with others" (Deci & Ryan, 2000, p. 253). We feel a sense of belonging and connectedness with others.

It is important to note here that Deci and Ryan's research does not suggest that happiness derived from support for autonomy comes from operating independently of others and in isolation. On the contrary, the research actually indicates that interdependence coupled with the ability to forge one's own destiny is the ultimate combination for fulfillment. More on this in chapter 3 (page 35).

You might be thinking that Self-Determination Theory is a *theory*—how do you know it will work for you in practice? It is a fair question. Let me share how support for autonomy, competence, and relatedness has influenced my own experiences in education—specifically in relation to the story I shared in the introduction. I became aware of how powerful it could be to support these three needs while reflecting on my experience implementing the turnaround model of school reform. It was through this experience I realized that not only did these three critical needs support growth and empowerment, but they also have the ability to restore and heal a school culture and the internal culture of educators as well.

Let me take you back to that afternoon in my school library when I was breaking the news of the turnaround model to my staff. The reality is that things did not suddenly get better. In fact, as I'm sure you can imagine, they got worse before they got better. I immediately began working with the elected interim leadership team to identify and develop the protocol for the subsequent interviews of all staff members. I then worked with the director of human resources and the assistant superintendent to conduct the interviews for more than fifty individuals all trying to salvage their positions as educators at the school—not to mention there were still three months of school left, and I had to monitor and ensure teachers stayed focused on instruction and their students' education in the midst of the turmoil.

It was a harrowing time for me. To this day, the gravity of what the turnaround model meant for those who were not selected to stay leaves me feeling unsettled.

The initial demands of setting up the turnaround model left me feeling demoralized by the system. I'll be completely honest: when I look back now, I realize how anxious I was at the time. Although I believed the forthcoming changes would have a positive impact on student achievement, I was also resentful of the whole process that we as educators had to go through to arrive at our starting point. I initially had feelings of frustration and doubt. Would the turnaround plan actually bring about the changes needed? Could I lead this staff to a school culture with restored relational trust while fostering the confidence and commitments absolutely necessary for any impactful change in student achievement?

Although there were times of doubt and frustration in the beginning, the good news is that, in the end, we accomplished great things; our doubts and frustration turned to a sense of pride and accomplishment. Together we created a strong and supportive school culture and utilized the PLC processes to keep focused on the right work for student success. Looking back now, I can see that much of our passion for our work and tenacity at the time related to the educators' abilities to fulfill their needs for autonomy, competence, and relatedness.

As we started implementing the turnaround model in the fall of 2010, my initial reflections brought me to the need for autonomy. Teachers are not the only ones faced with a lack of autonomy. School principals and leaders also find themselves having to carry out the mandates and policies of their state department of education and district. Leaders are susceptible to the same demoralizing effects teachers feel when asked to carry out initiatives they do not understand or are not committed to. School leaders often have to lead initiatives we don't support or don't have time to implement effectively before being judged for our progress and success. Yet in implementing the turnaround model, autonomy showed up as a gift that served to enhance self-efficacy and empowerment.

When the school improvement initiatives of 2009 began, autonomy was a big part of the package. The principals in the schools that were identified as performing lowest in their states were supposed to be given permission to think and act outside of the status quo box. In fact, we were expected to do so. Certainly, there were guidelines. One was that we must capitalize on researched practices of proven effectiveness. However, moving beyond the status quo and taking action was the call of the day. Unfortunately, many schools implementing school reform were not given autonomy; instead, state or district leaders dictated implementation of models of reform they had very little input in selecting. I, however, was given autonomy. My superintendent allowed me and my staff to forge our path and shielded us from anyone or anything that threatened to get in our way or question our direction.

As a result, my staff and I responded with enthusiasm. Guided by the action-oriented PLC culture, we were able to evaluate our school practices, examine our curriculum and assessments, research those practices that were yielding the highest benefits for students, and then implement them to impact student achievement at our school site. For me, this autonomy was part of the healing path of my own internal culture and definitely helped restore my sense of well-being and fulfillment. I do acknowledge, however, that while I had autonomy, this is not always the case. In chapter 3 (page 35), we will talk more about how to secure autonomy even when your superiors do not readily support it.

The turnaround model and the PLC commitment to a focus on results have helped fulfill my need to feel a sense of competence. It began with a commitment to focus on the results of school data on state assessments and a commitment to look squarely in the face of our current reality. After some debate, my leadership team and I decided to hold a parent night at the beginning of our first year in turnaround that would focus on clearly delineating for our parents and school community the current reality of our school standing as indicated by our state assessment results. It wasn't a pretty picture at the time and we weren't sure how this would go over, or if this was really the best way to start the school year. However, we all knew that a focus on results was one of our common commitments and imperative to our success, so we jumped in with both feet to bring the parents in on this commitment as well. As it turns out, truth is a very powerful motivator. We did a presentation that night that clearly informed parents that only 22 percent of students in the school could read and write at grade level and only 18 percent showed proficiency in mathematics in the prior school year. Apparently, this information had never been clearly and intentionally presented to our predominantly Spanish-speaking parents. To our relief, although this news shocked many, instead of being outraged at the results, the parents and community used this information as a rallying cry for better outcomes for their children. They were willing to join us in our commitment to ensure increased academic proficiency for their children and put their trust in us as we promised to do everything we could to change the trajectory for their children.

From here we began the process of setting goals, creating action plans, and then monitoring those plans as they began to make a difference in student achievement. Data and data analysis permeated our collaborative meetings, the walls of our classrooms and hallways, and the pages of student data notebooks as a tool that we used regularly to determine if students were learning. Collective evaluation of the results of our actions was built into our school culture, and we were attentive and responsive to what the data told us through a schoolwide response to intervention. Data encouraged us to act swiftly by showing us when students did or did not learn and were a barometer of the effectiveness of our practices. This focus gave us predictable feedback on our competence to effect change for our students and to build on those successes. Our sense of self-efficacy as educators began to increase as we witnessed students' academic successes and achieved proficiency rates higher than the school had seen since its inception. In just the second year of our work together, we were recognized as a Top Growth School in our state, and by the fourth year we had increased proficiency rates by 20 percent in both reading and mathematics on state assessments. Without question, this attention to setting goals, monitoring data, and celebrating successes brought with it strong feelings of competence.

Collaboration was a collective commitment from the start. Each educator who interviewed for a job at our school during the turnaround was asked about his or her commitment to collaboration and was told he or she would be working daily with a collaborative team. There was no question that building collaborative teams and relational trust through common commitments and norms of engagement was a foundation crucial to our success. We didn't identify it as *relatedness* at the time, but this is exactly what collaboration required and supported. We immediately started the process of identifying our mission, vision, values, and goals. The energy and collective input that went into these tasks were the initial steps in the healing process that would provide the courage needed to move forward with confidence. For myself, my guiding coalition not only supported the governing and decision-making processes of the school's shared leadership, but they also became trusted colleagues and friends. There were many times during our journey together that we needed social and emotional support. As a leader, I realized I, too, needed to feel supported and cared for. If it were not for this group of individuals, as well as the collective staff and community's support, I'm not sure how I would have fared as their leader. It is true that we all need to feel supported and cared for through relatedness regardless of our position of leadership. The collaborative culture, teams, and norms a PLC supports not only impacted student learning, but also supported the educators' need for connection and care as they pursed their goals to improve student outcomes.

I'm not sure we were aware at the time that having the structures, processes, and culture of the PLC would lead us on a journey that simultaneously put students' learning first while nurturing all three of these innate needs for motivation and well-being in ourselves. However, looking back, I'm even more certain the PLC process helped us survive in the high-stress environment of school reform. It fortified our courage to reach outside the box of what had been tried before. It supported feelings of competence as we watched data show increases for our students. It guided us to build the professional and personal relationships that would bolster us in the tough times and guide us toward the celebrations of our successes in the good times. And I am absolutely convinced the tenets of the PLC can do the same thing for you.

Building a Framework

The PLC model is one of the few systematic models of school reform that, at its core, honors educators as the intellectual masters of the educational profession. Its tenets and subsequent processes ensure that systems are set up so educators—those with the knowledge and skills to impact the changes that will close achievement gaps and ensure that all students achieve at high levels—are afforded the time and resources to achieve this goal. The model speaks directly to the research identified in the introduction that tells us that educators must be included in the decision-making and problem-solving processes if they are to feel motivated to act differently and effect positive change. The PLC model also ensures that the innate human needs for autonomy, competence, and relatedness are valued and supported.

In the next three chapters, I will identify how the culture, processes, and systems of the PLC foster, and in many ways ensure, a healthy internal culture for educators. The PLC model not only keeps educators focused on those things that actually impact student success, it concurrently keeps us focused on the things that support the internal culture of the educator. With this in mind, let's explore how the three big ideas of the PLC framework impact the well-being and motivation of educators by supporting the three innate needs identified in Self-Determination Theory.

> **Three Big Ideas of a Professional Learning Community**
>
> 1. Educators have an unwavering belief that all students can learn at high levels and will do whatever it takes to ensure this for their students (autonomy).
>
> 2. Educators understand that the only way to ensure all students learn at high levels is to work together to that end, in collaborative teams, with collective commitments (relatedness).
>
> 3. Educators have a relentless focus on results to ensure that what they are doing will bring about the intended learning outcomes for their students (competence).

A Focus on Learning

The first big idea is that all students can learn at high levels—not that they can be *taught* at high levels, but that they can *learn* at high levels. This idea keeps us focused on the moral imperative to ensure all students learn at high levels and fosters the belief systems that support it. It reminds us that it is *our* responsibility to ensure students learn at high levels, not the responsibility of a program or a textbook. The support of this belief beckons us to engage in active research to improve student outcomes through cycles of ongoing inquiry and implementations that lead to increased achievement for our students. It supports our need for autonomous action; those actions that provide us with opportunities for choice, creativity, and innovation.

A Collaborative Culture

The second big idea supports the belief that it is only through your collaborative efforts that you can accomplish great things for yourselves and your students. As you meet collectively to identify the current reality of student learning, you are able to bring your unique gifts and talents to the table. This collaboration allows you to move swiftly to help determine ways in which you can increase student learning, close the gaps of low achievement, and work collectively to meet your common goals. This expectation that you must meet collaboratively and share your knowledge in the pursuit of common goals meets your innate need for relatedness. As you work together and build on successes, a relational trust begins to form that brings with it a sense of caring, safety, and connectedness.

A Focus on Results

The third big idea in a PLC is that educators must stay focused on results. They have to know for sure that what they are doing is working. In a PLC, this is not an exercise in futility, where your reflections on student data serve only to remind you that your students are failing. The data in a PLC collaborative team become its motivation and battle cry. The data you look at are relevant and call you to respond immediately when students do not learn. Teams are not afraid of data; to the contrary, it is the data that motivate them to set goals, respond, create a plan of action, adapt that plan when necessary, and then celebrate their accomplishments. This pattern of collective inquiry that calls you to action and facilitates successes in turn creates feelings of competence in your work as educators.

If you have had the opportunity to work within a PLC that focuses on these three big ideas, you understand their inherent minimalist genius for ensuring student learning. If we let these beliefs drive everything we do when we work with students, it's difficult to go wrong. These three big ideas will inevitably put us on the path that we all desire in education—to achieve high levels of learning for all of our students. What you may not have considered before is how these same three big ideas also support your internal culture as an educator.

Unfortunately, PLCs are often implemented like many other top-down mandates, which don't necessarily build a common understanding about what outcome is actually intended. Many schools and districts that say they are working as PLCs maintain a too-tight form of leadership and preserve a fear-based form of management that seeks to control educators instead of empowering them. Those implementing the PLC often have little understanding of what a PLC actually is or what its members are committed to do. As a result, districts and schools using this top-down approach never really experience how the PLC framework can support high degrees of self-efficacy, confidence, and professional satisfaction for the teachers while at the same time creating successful academic and social outcomes for students. Many districts, schools, and educators consider the term *PLC* just another euphemism for a teacher meeting or holding staff meetings rather than defining a team of mutually accountable educators who come together to work interdependently toward common goals for student achievement (DuFour et al., 2016). However, as we clarify the educational dynamic that participants act on and protect in a PLC, and show how this work restores teacher self-efficacy, I guarantee that *PLC* will never again mean *a meeting* in your lexicon of educational terms. Instead, you will leave with a clear understanding of the comprehensive impact it has on students, educators, and education as a whole.

In the next three chapters, we will look closely at autonomy (chapter 3, page 35), competence (chapter 4, page 45), and relatedness (chapter 5, page 67), and at how working collectively as a PLC supports each of these needs, and in doing so, nurtures the internal culture of the educator as well. See figure 2.1.

	Autonomy	**Competence**	**Relatedness**
PLC at Work	• Action Research • Tight and Loose Leadership • Continuous Improvement	• Focus on Results • SMART Goals • Celebrations	• Collaborative Team • Relational Trust • Shared Leadership

FIGURE 2.1: PLC at Work supports for the internal culture of the educator.

Reflection

Before moving on, take time for some reflective writing. I'd like you to do the same thing I did when I learned about the three essential human needs of autonomy, competence, and relatedness; I reflected on times in my career that supported and enhanced these three essential needs in my work and thought about the subsequent outcomes. Take a moment to think about a time in your educational career where one or all of these innate needs were supported in some manner. Then, answer the three following questions via reflective writing.

1. Identify a time you felt a sense of autonomy in determining how you would act or respond to a challenge or opportunity in your career. What

were the circumstances around this time in your career? How did it make you feel?

2. Think about a time when you felt competent in what you put your intentions toward accomplishing in education. Again, what were the circumstances around this time in your career? Again, how did it make you feel?

3. Finally, consider the times in your profession when you had a sense of relatedness—times when you knew that you were not alone and when you felt supported and connected to others on your journey. When was this? What were the circumstance? How did it feel? Did it bring a sense of well-being to your life as an educator?

As you go through the next few chapters, hold on to these recollections. They will reinforce the importance of your work in this process toward restoring your hope in public education and empower you to take action for your students. Research suggests that by rehearsing your successes, your mindset becomes better calibrated to take on the next set of challenges with an attitude of confidence while producing higher rates of success (Taylor & Pham, 1999).

One other important idea that I want you to hold in your awareness as you move through this book is your *why* statement.

Revisiting Your *Why*

Simon Sinek's (2011) groundbreaking book *Start With Why* and his viral TED Talk in 2010 on the same subject, examine the need to start your work in any organization with the *why* of what you do. Sinek suggests that your *why* has to be secure before you can engage in the *how* and *what* of your organization or field. By getting back to the reason you entered this profession in the first place, you get back to your core. It is in that core place that you find your renewed passion. In your quest to nurture the three innate needs identified in SDT—autonomy, competence, and relatedness—securing your *why* paves your way. So, I ask you to do one more reflective writing exercise before we move on.

Because this is such an important foundation for your work, I ask that you find a time and place where you won't be interrupted and give this exercise your complete attention.

Sinek, Peter Docker, and David Mead (2017) aptly state, "If we want to feel an undying passion for our work, if we want to feel we are contributing to something bigger than ourselves, we all need to know our *why*" (p. 21). Getting back to your reasons for being an educator may be one of the most important exercises in this book. So, let's consider a few more questions. After reading each one, take time to write down your thoughts.

1. Write a short paragraph or two about your journey to becoming an educator. Did you know from an early age you wanted to be an educator working with students? Did you come to this desire later in life? What path did you take that led you to where you are now as an educator?

2. What is it about your job that makes you feel most rewarded, both personally and professionally? What part of your job makes you feel most personally and professionally empowered?

3. What strengths do you bring to your profession as an educator? What are the innate or hard-earned strengths that you contribute?

4. How do you measure your success as an educator?

My hope is that these questions will offer a clearer understanding of what drives you as an educator. Maybe some other questions came up for you in this reflection; if so, I encourage you to explore them, too. Again, take your time with these questions so that you develop an authentic response to this prompt.

My *Why* Statement

I choose to be an educator at this time in my life, at this time in history, because . . .

_____

_____

Once you have your *why* statement, give it a place of honor. Perhaps you might feature it on your computer screensaver. Maybe you set it to pop up on your calendar once a week or put a sticky note on your mirror in the morning so you can reflect on it before you head out the door. Whatever you decide, make sure you set yourself up to revisit this statement frequently so it can empower and motivate you as you move forward.

3

Autonomy

Autonomy. Just the sound of the word rolling off the tongue brings visions of freedom and empowerment. It's not surprising that autonomy has been found to be such an important part of fulfillment and well-being. As living, breathing, thinking, and creating human beings, it makes sense that being able to determine our trajectories toward our desired outcomes in our professions and in our personal lives is inevitably linked to happiness. Deci and Ryan's (2008) research suggests that we need autonomy in our lives not only because research supports the idea to be self-directed when pursuing personal goals, but because the desire for autonomy and self-direction has also been shown to be innate—not just for some but for all. So, in this chapter we are going to clarify the norms and attributes of those organizations that support autonomy for their members and the subsequent impact of that support on educators. Then we will correlate how the PLC culture of action research and shared leadership provides these very supports for educators.

One question that may arise is, How did education move so far from the systems and processes that support autonomy for educators in the first place?

Control leads to compliance; autonomy leads to engagement.

—Daniel H. Pink

Find the autonomy in your work. Autonomy is key to feeling good about the work you do, no matter what kind of work it is.

—Jean Chatzky

How did so many in our profession find themselves feeling disempowered and, as a result, unmotivated and victimized? Some attribute this situation to the relentless focus on high-stakes testing that came out of the No Child Left Behind and the Race to the Top eras of educational policy. It appears that high-stakes standardized tests and the accompanying rewards and punishments are now permanently etched into the culture of public education. With pressure to conform to testing policies and rating systems for schools and districts, decision makers in public education somehow decided to stop trusting teachers. Instead, they started putting blind trust in programs and curriculums touted as a quick route to ensure high achievement for all students. This may seem an oversimplification of the problem, and granted, it certainly doesn't show the whole picture. However, *teacher-proofing* schools—a concept based in the idea that the content of a curriculum is more important to learning than an educator who knows how to present it effectively—is a primary focus in the industry of school reform. The educational funding that is directed toward curriculum and assessment publishers and private organizations sweeping in with proposed cure-alls for school reform efforts is well documented and, whether intentional or not, is supporting the continued adherence to this underlying belief system that teachers cannot be trusted to do their work as professionals without top-down control (Merrow, 2017). As Daniel Pink (2009) so eloquently presents in his book *Drive: The Surprising Truth About What Motivates Us*, the outdated systems of top-down, control-based modes of management and leadership, those that squelch creativity and enforce compliance, have failed organizations for years.

Action Research

On an encouraging note, research is beginning to pave the way to a new paradigm. The power of having employees work interdependently to discover proactive problem-solving approaches to generate innovative solutions has gained traction. In a PLC, we call this *action research*, in which educators work interdependently to act on their knowledge and insights about what will work to improve learning outcomes for their students. In action research, educators identify a plan of action, identify how they will measure the success of their innovations—then they act! By evaluating their results along the way, they either celebrate and expand a successful practice they initiated, or adapt their strategy to achieve better results. Sharing the positive results of their action research with their collaborative teams and colleagues is also an expectation. This kind of action research can only come about when schools, districts, and communities empower educators to set goals and think about how to achieve them while creating an environment that supports their autonomy.

Autonomy Supports

A study conducted by Baard, Deci, and Ryan in 2004 looks at employees working in the investment banking industry—a very different profession from education, but the study has applications for educators nonetheless. This study compared two groups: one group of employees was given *autonomy supports* (see figure 3.1) throughout the study, while the other group maintained a top-down, business-as-usual management style. The study's autonomy supports included leaders and managers offering their workers control over what actions to take and how to implement them when meeting established workplace goals and objectives. Managers also encouraged employees to communicate their points of view and acknowledged the value in receiving their views. They encouraged their employees to initiate their own course of action, offering feedback intended to inform, rather than manipulate, these actions. At the end of the study, the research found that employees given these autonomy supports not only reported higher job satisfaction, they also performed better and were more successful at their work. In addition, the employees indicated they felt more trust and comradery with their colleagues. Just these few simple supports for autonomy had the effect of increasing employee satisfaction and achieving organizational goals, which was good for both the employees *and* the company.

So how does this study apply to the field of public education? Let's take a look.

Autonomy Supports
- Having one's ideas and perspectives acknowledged
- Providing meaningful information in a non-manipulating manner
- Proving opportunities for choice
- Encouraging self-initiation

Source: Deci, Eghrari, Patrick, and Leone, 1994.

FIGURE 3.1: Autonomy supports.

Autonomy Support Number One—Having One's Ideas and Perspectives Acknowledged

The first autonomy support is having your ideas and perspectives acknowledged. The only way you can have your ideas and perspectives acknowledged is to share them. In a PLC, the fundamental structure of the school becomes the collaborative team in which teachers are expected to work interdependently to achieve common goals for which they are mutually accountable. When a school has developed a culture of relational trust and a strong belief that educators need one another to reach their goals, the individual educator's ideas are shared and reinforced each time the collaborative team meets. When teachers share common standards and work together to ensure all students are learning those standards, the ideas and innovations that come through collaborating around student work will demand that your knowledge and insights are shared, honored, and celebrated. This may make you feel vulnerable at first; however, once you step in and commit to sharing your insights with others, you will begin to understand and capitalize on the empowerment that comes through sharing your ideas and having them impact change for both yourself and those who benefit from your knowledge. No, you and your team are not always going to agree on how to move forward, but a common value is that all voices need to be heard and honored as the team moves toward a collective commitment to achieve more for our students.

Autonomy Support Number Two—Providing Meaningful Information in a Non-Manipulative Manner

What exactly does it mean to provide meaningful information in a *non-manipulative manner*? Let's first consider how information can be used in a manipulative manner. Suppose members of the state Department of Education or the district superintendent's office decide a certain curriculum or program will meet the state's or district's needs for remediation or effective first instruction. They invest in the curriculum, ideology, technology, or program they feel will transform their state or district. They then announce to the educators in their state or district, far too often in a disjointed manner, that schools and districts are to implement this new initiative with fidelity starting this year. Now, this initiative *may* have strong potential to fill an instructional need and close gaps in student achievement. The new initiative itself may actually offer benefits rather than cause problems. But problems arise when too little attention is given to the necessary education, information, and support—all of which are meaningful information—that educators need before they can embrace and implement the new initiative. Instead of involving school leaders and educators at the site level in making choices about a particular initiative, state and district decision makers move forward quickly without any significant input from the educators, who must carry out an initiative that's new to them with limited, if any, understanding of the decision-making process. So when school leaders and educators finally get the professional development and the subsequent expectations about implementation, they are mostly disengaged from the *why* of what they are doing.

In this scenario, information is given to educators *after* the decision has been made. The purpose of information transfer is not to build common commitments, ask for ideas, and get feedback, all of which should happen during the decision-making process. Instead, information is designed to manipulate *how* the educators act in the future, without including them in the determination of *why* they need to act that way to accomplish specific goals.

A less manipulative method for approaching this process would be to identify to educators what problems need solving and what limitations or constraints might exist, then ask the educators in each school or district to collaboratively develop recommendations for actions that fit within those constraints and use that feedback to develop a plan. Not all educators may like the plan or agree with all its aspects, but involvement in its development means they at least understand its purpose—its *why*—enabling them to implement it more effectively in their classrooms.

In situations where collaborative decision making isn't possible, decision makers in states and districts can provide meaningful information in a comprehensive, responsive way that allows educators to ask questions and develop an understanding of the project's goals. While this offers less autonomy and engagement, it at least supports the educators' ability to develop a sense of the *why* behind the initiative, rather than feel that they're simply being given arbitrary instructions on how to do their jobs from people distant from their daily realities.

Autonomy Support Number Three—Providing Opportunities for Choice

The need for choice is at the core of what we think of when we think of autonomy. Let's assume for a moment that all educators have an unwavering belief in the ability of all students to learn at high levels and that this belief drives them each day when they walk into the classroom. Even with this shared belief, there is no guarantee that they will all work out a similar path to enact the belief. Often, different ideas about how to move forward lead to a power struggle instead of a celebration of ingenuity, insight, and talent. The beauty of the PLC processes is that they honor different and creative ideas as critical to the pathway to improve student learning and the foundation for how we can do things better. The idea of continuous improvement through the action research of the educators in the school is a core foundational belief. The knowledge that the work is never done and we are always learning how to do it better drives the PLC forward, and frankly, gives us purpose. With shared leadership as a core foundation, the PLC processes compel us to let go of the predominant culture of control, with its overuse of teacher-proof programs and curriculums, and put the power of change back in the hands of the educators. The collaborative culture of the PLC is set up with the explicit purpose of honoring choice in how teachers meet the school, team, and personal goals developed to achieve high levels of learning for their students. This culture encourages teachers to engage with new ideas, implement research-based practices, and to look closely at student results to see if their efforts are working for students.

Autonomy Support Number Four—Encouraging Self-Initiation

Encouraging the autonomy to self-initiate a plan to improve student learning and offering the time and resources to support this effort can be one of the greatest gifts for educators. However, educators potentially have two responses to the freedom to self-initiate: some educators have been waiting for this opportunity and can't wait to jump in, while others fear failure. The second group fears having to think outside the structures that have been part of the paradigm of *school* possibly since they entered kindergarten. The thinking is that if they stay within the structures of the traditional schedules and assigned curriculum of schooling, they will face less difficulty in performing their jobs.

Yet this research supports the assertion that when teachers are given the autonomy to create positive changes, and supported in those efforts, there is greater teacher satisfaction and more effective innovations as they work toward meeting their goal of higher levels of learning for their students. This autonomy support reinforces the idea that teachers need to be encouraged to step out of their comfort zones and grow their professional expertise.

Change can produce fear and anxiety for most of us. However, with the support of a PLC, change becomes safer. You are not in this alone; change is expected, and the PLC leadership and collaborative team give you the support you need to create positive changes for your students.

As we look at the attrition rate of teachers in our profession, the practice of autonomy support isn't just a good idea—it has become nonnegotiable. It is certainly not a time for teacher-proofing our schools. When we recognize the value of teacher insights and innovation, we will stop our schools from continuing down the unsettling path of educator burnout and unsuccessful school reform initiatives. Learning new ways of doing things and addressing student achievement through action research and discovery becomes imperative as we face the changing nature of education and identify the necessary skills students need to thrive in a 21st-century society. And, as promised, the PLC model of school improvement offers these very supports.

Tight and Loose Leadership

Having just talked about autonomy and empowerment, let me also introduce the concepts of *tight* and *loose* leadership. A PLC values the autonomy of the educator to discover and implement strategies that best meet the needs of the students in their classrooms. The loose part of the PLC process honors the action research imperative in the work of the PLC ethos. It represents the belief that the educators in the school have within them the answers to increasing student achievement, but they need autonomy to find them. Instead of mandates and manipulation, shared leadership and collective decision making determine the pedagogy, scheduling, curriculum, interventions, and assessments. Teachers are given the autonomy to question, give input, discover, and adapt. PLCs let data inform priorities and action steps.

Yet the autonomy supported in a PLC is by no means a free-for-all. Neither top-down micromanagement nor a chaotic, undisciplined style of management are effective. When we say *collective commitments*, we mean that everyone involved shares a commitment to the goals and practices in question. The entrepreneurial spirit of the educator is valued, but we also uphold research-based, solid practices in our daily promises to each other. As stated in *Learning by Doing* (DuFour et al., 2016), "high-performing PLCs avoid the too-tight/too loose trap by engaging educators in an improvement process that empowers them to make decisions at the same time that they require adherence to core elements of the process" (p. 14). Anyone who has been in education for any length of time knows that neither the too-loose nor the too-tight form of leadership works. Neither extreme can inspire or motivate. So, let's look at the following six nonnegotiables—the *tight* of a PLC—to clarify those practices and structures proven to have high leverage for increasing levels of academic achievement in schools.

Tight Elements of a PLC

1. Educators work collaboratively rather than in isolation, take collective responsibility for student learning, and clarify the commitments they make to each other about how they will work together.

2. The fundamental structure of the school becomes the collaborative team in which members work interdependently to achieve common goals for which all members are mutually accountable.

3. The team establishes a guaranteed and viable curriculum, unit by unit, so all students have access to the same knowledge and skills regardless of which teacher is assigned to their classroom.

4. The team develops common formative assessments to frequently gather evidence of student learning.

5. The school has created a system of interventions and extensions to ensure students who struggle receive additional time and support for learning in a way that is timely, directive, diagnostic, and systematic. Additionally, students who demonstrate proficiency can extend their learning.

6. The team uses evidence of student learning to inform and improve the individual and collective practice of its members (DuFour et al., 2016, p. 14).

After reading through these tight elements of a PLC, you may be wondering where, in all this discussion of teams and collaboration, the autonomy comes in. Remember, research on autonomy does not advocate a *go-it-alone, hope for the best* approach to initiatives in organizations. On the contrary, research indicates that supporting the nonnegotiables for your learning community provides autonomy to the educator in the pursuit of achieving goals outlined by the organization (Van den Broeck, Vansteenkiste, De Witt, Soenens, & Lens, 2010). As long as educators are provided with a meaningful rationale for following these tight practices and are given respect and choice in meeting expectations, their well-being and motivation are still nurtured and protected. In a PLC, it is the responsibility of the leadership to create the shared understanding of the *why* of those practices identified as tight, and to ensure the understanding is solid and the "will of the group" is understood collectively (DuFour et al., 2016, p. 32). This goes a long way in ensuring that the school community is able to move forward collectively and with a sense of autonomy.

Many educators have come to believe that a school culture where teachers are encouraged to expand their knowledge by questioning, problem-solving, learning from their outcomes, and making choices about how to respond to student needs—in short, educators' autonomy—has been lost. This is not true! The collective accountability and results-based practices of the PLC, as well as a culture of support for bringing more effective strategies to the table and challenging those practices that are not creating results for students, provide a safe environment to take on challenges and find a better way, even if that better way contains tight elements.

Some teachers may have actually been programmed to ignore the compulsion for autonomy and contributing to positive change through years of functioning in a culture that requires only compliance and being managed. After trying to give voice to what you think could be a better way to move forward, you're told instead to comply. After too many disappointments and frustrations, it's easy to say to yourself, "I give up. I'm just going to do what I'm told and let the chips fall where they may." This resignation can lead to a practice where you work hard in your own classroom, but avoid making yourself too vulnerable by trying to promote change for your team or school community. Or, you may have come from an educational experience where you were never expected to champion change. You've never been expected to be innovative and actively engaged in figuring out how to reach every student. Perhaps your introduction to your school went like this: you were given a schedule, possibly a scope and sequence for the prescribed curriculum, keys to your classroom, and a command to "hit the ground running." You were told to get through every unit of study by the end of the year as this was your best bet at educating students, but in reality, you're merely *covering* the curriculum. You may have fallen victim to the idea that *teaching* is our primary responsibility with *learning* becoming a secondary priority. While many new teachers feel comforted and even saved by these tools their first year or two in the classroom, this approach can only offer security for a short time. Eventually, the ineffectiveness of following a lockstep program or curriculum to meet the needs of *all* your students becomes glaringly evident. What was once a secure safety net becomes limiting to you and to your students. You quickly realize that not all students are learning, but no one seems to have any urgency about addressing the issue.

In a PLC culture, everything we do focuses on ensuring all students are learning at high levels. A PLC, at its heart, focuses on change, which requires self-initiative. As researcher and professor of education Andy Hargreaves correctly asserts, "When a school becomes a professional learning community, everything in the school looks different than it did before" (quoted in Sparks, 2004, p. 48). This is the power of individual and collective autonomy.

Reflection

Let's stop for a reflection on autonomy. I have identified two sets of related questions that I'd like you to consider in preparation for the actions we will take in chapter 6 (page 97).

1. What actions or practices have you as a teacher, support specialist, or administrator, wanted to implement in your classroom, school, or district but, for whatever reason, put off? What intuitive *ah-ha* moments have you come to in your practice that you feel would make a positive difference in student academic achievement, dispositions, and successes if you were to act on them?

2. Does a body of research exist about your ideas that you can tap into? What do your colleagues think about the innovation? If you have good evidence that this idea has the potential to impact student learning, what is it? Go ahead and write it down, or make a list if you have several ideas.

Now, let's look at your responses. If your idea doesn't have any explicit, immediate risk or harm, you likely can implement it in some form—even if it is just you in your classroom, or a small pilot group of teachers—that will allow you to track its success and effectiveness and share the results with your colleagues. Thus, while you may have to continue to follow the *tight* of your school or district, you can begin to make an impact based on your autonomy to act. This is so important for the health of your internal culture as an educator.

At this point, the discussion has covered why educators need to have the autonomy to act. The next step is to revisit how identifying intentions and goals based on your autonomy to act as an educator, and tracking the progress your goals are making toward student success, support your innate need to feel competent in your craft as educators.

4

Competence

When I first started working with schools in different areas of the United States, I was surprised by the number of educators I spoke with who conveyed feelings of incompetence about their work. The sentiment was not isolated to one region or one type of school. Although the educators I spoke with were sincerely trying to make a difference in the lives of their students, they felt as if they just weren't meeting the mark—at least academically. They felt like good soldiers trying to do what was expected of them but lacked confidence that they were making the verifiable impact on student learning that would allow them to truly feel good about their work as educators.

To feel competent about the work one is doing is a critical component of supporting and strengthening the internal culture of the educator. Competence and self-efficacy go hand in hand. In this chapter, we will look at the difference between a pattern of compliance versus passion-driven efforts to create an authentic plan to achieve results for our students. In the context of the PLC, we will look at how setting goals and tracking progress toward the achievement

Believe in yourself! Have faith in your abilities! Without a humble but reasonable confidence in your own powers you cannot be successful or happy.

—Norman Vincent Peale

of those goals help reclaim your sense of competency as educators and improve outcomes for your students. This perspective supports the belief systems and processes that ensure educators are collectively making the decisions about how to respond to student needs.

Recognizing and Addressing a Sense of Incompetence

Why do so many educators feel a sense of incompetence when it comes to making a difference, particularly for our most struggling students? There are many reasons that can be attributed to feelings of incompetence in our profession, but one factor in particular needs highlighting: many initiatives intended to encourage competency are actually doing just the opposite. Let me illustrate this point by telling you about Alex, a principal at a middle school in a midsized district in the Southwest.

When I met Alex, he was looking for support to achieve the goal of becoming a high-performing PLC. During one of my initial visits, I met with Alex and his English language arts (ELA) teacher team to look at their current data to identify causes for continued low performance in ELA state assessment scores. I asked them to look at the data with an eye for what they thought might be root causes for low achievement rates in their ELA classes. Some of the first responses that came up were, "Well, it's hard when the kids just don't care," or "If they don't come to school, what can we expect?" and, "They came to us with low academic skills. What are we supposed to do? We're not miracle workers!"

As you can see, there was an obvious cultural issue at the school, as teachers were more likely to deflect responsibility than roll up their sleeves and get to work figuring out how they could close the obvious achievement gaps. This is certainly not the first time I've heard this defense. In fact, I hear similar statements from educators far and wide. What I've come to understand about many of the educators who give these reasons for low student achievement is that they are not necessarily callous teachers. Instead, they just continually find themselves in a place where they feel stuck and don't know what to do. Often, when a person feels stuck or too paralyzed to take action, it can be an indicator that he or she fears being incompetent. This is a difficult place to be when you are an educator.

Often, educators have diligently applied all the curriculums and programs they have been asked to implement. They have followed the curriculum map and pacing guides. They have looked at large bodies of data and filled out all the accountability graphs and paperwork required by their districts. However, it never seems to change anything. Student achievement data stay stagnant. One factor contributing to this stagnation in schools and districts is the programs and curriculums they are asked to implement to change patterns of low achievement are themselves constantly changing. Alex and his team were an example of this pattern of ever-changing initiatives that often leads to feelings of incompetence—even if they may be hidden feelings.

As my conversation with Alex and his teachers continued, I asked them to dig a little deeper. I wanted them to try and find the authentic cause of their frustrations and the continued low achievement for their students. As they began to share their reflections, a common root cause of teacher apathy began to surface: constantly shifting priorities and expectations. It was the school instructional coach, Cindy, who laid it out on the table for all to see. She described a series of initiatives the district had introduced over the last five years regarding the *best* strategies and curriculum to improve ELA achievement scores in the district. She recalled that when she first became an instructional coach, she had great enthusiasm for her work. She felt excited about supporting her school, the teachers, and the district. The current director of curriculum and instruction's plan for increasing student achievement for middle school students seemed solid to her, and she carried the torch for implementation with fidelity. The focus for middle schools was a recently purchased curriculum that was presented as the best data-based curriculum available for providing quality instruction to Tiers I, II, and III. It came from a well-known publisher and had been updated to include literature sure to capture the middle school reader's attention, scaffolded prompts and lessons to reach students at all levels, and a suite of technology programs to support teacher and student learning. She and her fellow instructional coaches were poised to train all district middle school ELA teachers in the new curriculum. They also developed pacing guides that would be monitored for fidelity.

As Cindy recalled this initiative, I saw heads nod with collective recognition of the time and the initiative. They all agreed that, as with any new curriculum adoption, there was a steep learning curve. The first year was challenging for teachers as they dug into new lessons, strategies, and technology. First there was some resistance to the new curriculum; however, they all agreed that the following year came with a little more confidence and a little more buy-in. And, even though there was no significant increase in student achievement after the first year, teachers were more hopeful that they could implement the curriculum with a refined expertise that would bring about more positive outcomes for students during the next school year. Cindy indicated this created a sense of accomplishment and hope for her.

Midway through the second year, however, the director of curriculum and instruction announced her retirement and a new director was hired for the following year. This new director had a commitment to an entirely different program and philosophy to turn around the low proficiency rates in middle schools. And with this change, a new curriculum and instructional focus were implemented that went in an entirely different direction. Cindy shared her initial shock and confusion. She had just spent the last two years building commitment and common understanding in the curriculum touted as the best way to meet the needs of all learners. Now she was being asked to take her teachers in an entirely new direction! She did not hesitate to convey to us her frustration at the system that supported leaders and programs more than the knowledge and insights of administrators and teachers in the schools and classrooms. The year I began working with this school, another director of curriculum and instruction was appointed, shifting the focus once again. As Cindy concluded her story, I learned that the present initiatives actually lacked buy-in from most of the teachers. Again, heads in the room nodded in agreement while other individuals in the meeting shared similar frustrations.

As I spoke with this team, I realized they had no real understanding about what direction to move in. Many teachers were using different programs than their colleagues, and none had common expectations for student outcomes. They felt stuck and incompetent to move forward confidently. They were waiting for the district to tell them what to do.

Unfortunately, this often happens in public education. No doubt this is how the sarcastic phrase, "What will be the next flavor of the day?" became a common response from educators faced with yet another new initiative. Whether district leaders understand the impact of these inconsistent, here-today, gone-tomorrow decisions or not, teachers in schools most certainly do. It was very apparent that the educators I met with that day felt that precious time had been lost, and they felt incompetent because the achievement gaps in their district continued to be glaring. In this case, their feelings of incompetence had led them to start blaming the students, evident in comments such as, "The kids don't care" and "They come to us with low academic skills."

This is just one of the many examples that illustrate how easily we can find ourselves feeling incompetent and even demoralized by continued inconsistencies in the things we are asked to implement as educators. Instead of nurturing and supporting a strong belief and trust in the educators teaching our children, the culture of public education has moved toward searching for answers outside of the school. With this faulty focus, public education has neglected to set up the systems and processes to ensure educators are actively and consistently participating in the decisions about those resources and strategies that will bring success to students and build the educator's sense of *competence*. But even in less than ideal circumstances, we do not have to fall victim to this thinking ourselves. We can shift the focus from blame (which leads to inaction) and instead take actions that empower you and your colleagues to discover ways to create positive outcomes for both you and your students. It requires educators to become knowledgeable and intimately engaged with their outcomes, and if they are not producing success for students, they commit to doing whatever it takes to turn this trend around—even if it requires challenging the status quo. This can show up in many different ways: curriculum changes, schedule changes, increased training on effective pedagogy, a collective plan of response when students do or do not learn content standards. It can even be a call to organize and bring voice to ineffective mandates at the district and state levels. Whatever your school decides is necessary, it should be done with consensus and collective commitments to ensure that educators are meeting their moral imperative to do whatever it takes to ensure learning for all.

I'm happy to report Alex and his ELA teachers committed to taking collective action to align their curriculum and collective commitments. After realizing that lack of commitment and ultimately confusion about what direction to take were standing in the way of improving student outcomes, the team began the process of creating an action plan that would guide them toward a consistent curriculum alignment and response to intervention. The plan included steps to identify essential standards and learning targets, create units of instruction to ensure these essential standards were a priority in the curriculum map, and create common formative assessments that focused on rigor and would give information on how to quickly respond when students struggled to learn essential standards and how to develop enrichment when students mastered the standards. These initial action steps allowed the teachers to bring consistency to their curriculum and ensure all students had access to essential learnings and instruction.

They stopped waiting for someone outside the school to tell them what to do; instead, realizing those outside the school seemed more confused about what to do than even they were, they decided to take responsibility for evaluating current practices and implementing the resources and strategies they decided would best meet the needs of their students. They recognized the expertise present in the school and began to create action steps they knew would work with their students. In the process, they found that they felt more competent than ever before.

Turning the Tide: Setting Goals for Competence and Increased Self-Efficacy

Educators can chart a new path, particularly in relation to the innate need to feel competent in their work. One step to take immediately is to set a course of action to reclaim your power and build your sense of competence again. In doing so, you start the path to increased well-being and contentment in your profession—regardless of the public education culture in which you find yourself.

You might be thinking, "That sounds great, but how am I supposed to do it?" It's a good question. One of the very first steps you can take is to revisit your *why*—as you have already begun doing through the reflective writing exercise outlined earlier in the book. You may have already placed your *why statement* in a prominent spot where you see it in your day-to-day life. You may already feel it influencing you as a source of inspiration renewal. This is good. You are starting to create an environment and circumstances to not only produce a cycle of student success, but also a feeling of competence that heals your internal culture as an educator. "But what about concrete steps forward?" you may ask. "How does one move from inspiration to action and then to achievement?" Setting SMART goals is one way to take definitive steps forward.

Setting SMART Goals

Goal setting has developed a bad reputation in education. Often, attempts to create goals that are *specific, measurable, attainable, results oriented,* and *time bound*—or SMART (O'Neill & Conzemius, 2013; see also Drucker, 2008, and Doran,

1981)—are met with a mindset of compliance as opposed to intention. Yet goal setting holds the power to turn us from a focus on victimization and blaming to feelings of empowerment and success—success that allows us to take control of our circumstances and to take our places again as the leaders in our profession. Goals are the precursor to action, and it is only through action that we find our successes and reinforce our sense of competence. Although some educators may have never set concrete goals for work in education, many work in schools and districts where they are asked to set goals for success at least once a year, particularly if they are required to complete a school-improvement plan.

So, you may be saying to yourself, "OK, we've done the whole SMART goal thing before. It doesn't do anything to make me feel any better." I hear this a lot. Why does goal setting in the school culture fail to make us feel good about our work? First, as mentioned previously, we often do it out of compliance, not from a place of passion or urgency about our intended outcomes. You should feel intimately connected to your goals in such a way that you are compelled to visit them often and evaluate your progress toward meeting them. If your goals occupy a folder on your computer that you never open instead of being front and center in your thoughts and your work environment, then they most likely are not goals that will drive changes or lead to the successes you are seeking. And if you have set goals in your profession that have not produced outcomes that you celebrate and that don't motivate you every time you step into the school, then you may need to rethink how you have engaged in the process of goal setting.

There is no question that goal setting has a positive impact on one's self-efficacy, feelings of competence, and sense of well-being. In their 2006 research article, "New Directions in Goal-Setting Theory," Edwin Locke and Gary Latham state that "goals set the primary standard for self-satisfaction with performance" (p. 265). This is exactly where we want to go to build a continued source of competence. So, look at goal setting as a way of nurturing your competence. Consider goal setting as having the potential to bring more confidence and satisfaction to your work as an educator because meeting goals set to improve student outcomes also builds our own competency and expertise. This may not be the way goal setting has been presented to you in the past, but looking at your educational goals as a way to help increase your competence levels does not imply you're being selfish and putting the students in your care or their academic results on the back burner—you're not! The passion of the educator to ensure all students learn at high levels drives improved achievement. When educators claim their power to do what's right for students and take individual and collective responsibility for achieving these goals, we all win!

Goal setting is not merely the act of creating goals. As with any tool introduced into our practice, it is our commitment and passion to the actions that goal setting promotes that give the goals transformational power. So don't wait for some outside influence to guide your steps toward moving the academic achievement needle in the positive direction for you and your students. Take action! You may not be able to control the circumstances of your state or district, or even your school, at the moment. But no one can take away your ability to create a vision of success for yourself, your team, and your students, and then set the goals to achieve it.

What Makes a Goal SMART?

We start by revisiting (or for some of you, introducing) the SMART goal. It's not the only way to set a goal, but it's a pretty good model that has stood the test of time as a construct for goal setting.

The SMART goal format developed in the field of business management; the acronym SMART debuted in a 1981 *Management Review* article by George T. Doran. Doran's main focus in this article is to build on the goal-setting practices spelled out by well-known business management expert Peter Drucker (2008) in his landmark management textbook (originally published 1973) by introducing a more effective and consistent way to set and monitor goals in the business context. Doran felt that setting the SMART parameters was the only way to determine if the stated objectives of a company or organization were actually moving them closer to their desired outcomes. Doran felt that organizations were identifying objectives, yet no one was really monitoring whether or how employees or business units were meeting the intended objectives. Doran saw a tendency for goal setting to be ambiguous because there was really no designated way to align goals, set criteria for evaluating the goal, and then communicate those goals to others. He found that most companies were not effectively monitoring objectives, so they were not really impacting change. (Sound familiar?) It was out of this disconnect between goals and outcomes that the SMART goal process was born.

The term *SMART goal* has become an innocuous staple in many educators' vocabularies. You've heard of them, and you've most likely written them. Yet too often these SMART goals never really lead to any actions that are different from what you were doing before you wrote the goal. Again, they are too often created out of a need for compliance instead of out of passion to impact change (a recipe for failure from the get-go). It is important to change that pattern. The goals you create not only support student learning, but also support your internal culture as an educator—for example, your sense of competency and, as a result, your sense of empowerment.

So let's explore SMART goals. Basically, a SMART goal is developed using the criteria shown in figure 4.1. To be SMART, a goal must contain the following elements represented in the figure.

S—Specific
M—Measurable
A—Attainable
R—Results Oriented
T—Time Bound

FIGURE 4.1: SMART goal-setting parameters.

You often find SMART goals in school-improvement plans or on state, district, or school websites. Take this one, for example:

> By the end of the 2018–2019 academic year, students at Southwest Middle School in grades 6–8 will increase the number of students scoring Exceeding/Ready by 10 percent in Reading from 56 percent to 66 percent as demonstrated by ACT Aspire assessment data.

Now, let's determine if this goal meets the criteria for a SMART goal:

- Is it a specific goal?—Yes, it measures students' proficiency in reading skills.
- Is it measurable?—Yes, an increase of 10 percent of the students demonstrating proficiency on the state assessment measuring reading ability can be measured.
- Is it attainable?—If the staff and stakeholders in the school creating this goal looked carefully at the data and were able to evaluate the needs and actions necessary to meet those needs, then yes.

- Is it results oriented?—Yes, they want 66 percent of their students to be proficient in reading skills.
- Is it time bound?—Yes, they want to create these conditions by the end of the 2018–2019 academic year.

It appears that this goal does indeed meet the criteria of a SMART goal. Does this look familiar to you? Presumably, it does. However, the next question is, Have writing goals like this produced any changes in your actions or those of your team? Too often, the answer is *no*. I'm not suggesting that these goals are not important; however, the act of writing them alone doesn't produce the intended outcomes identified in the goal. We have to find ways to connect to the school's goals in personal and passionate ways.

Goal Setting for Change on the Individual Level

In my experience, this passion can come through setting both the individual teacher's goals and the collaborative team goals that align with the schoolwide goals. Although we will talk about both collective and individual goal setting, I want to start by looking at individual goal setting and how this impacts engagement and increased feelings of competence for the educator. Let me introduce a story about one educator, Derick, who used individual goal setting to build his sense of competency and autonomy of action while also working toward his school's collaborative goals.

Derick worked in a Title I school that had recently gone through a restructuring process with the intent of "shaking things up." The state test data for the school's students had shown no improvement during the two-year time frame for success outlined in the state's policies for school improvement. The new restructuring, mandated by the district and implemented at the beginning of the school year, required replacement of the current principal, as the school had not met the SMART goals outlined in the school-improvement plan during her tenure. The replacement was required even though evidence showed they were making great cultural strides and systems were being set up for change. Because teachers and staff had committed to and believed in the vision they had created with the outgoing principal, many educators in the building were shocked by this development and resented this seemingly reckless decision to remove their principal. As a result, the morale in the school's staff plummeted.

While the loss of the former principal affected everyone, it seemed to weigh particularly heavy on Derick, who was newly hired at the school when the new principal took over. Although Derick was not familiar with the former principal and vision, he found the negativity in the building was definitely having an impact on him. In addition to the unrest of his colleagues, Derick's sense of anxiety was exasperated by his sense of isolation. He was the only teacher in his grade level and feared he would not meet the required growth set forth in the school's improvement plan for his grade. Add to this the implementation of four new, mandated programs that were to be executed simultaneously. Derick felt out of his depth and feared he, too, would be susceptible to losing his job.

Many factors contributed to Derick's feeling of being overwhelmed. One of the factors is a common mistake in schools: initiative fatigue. This mistake is often precipitated by the sudden influx of large sums of money to improve student performance. The school or district, in an attempt to use all the money allocated, begins buying programs, professional development, and curriculums that the publishers or developers promise will meet the needs of their low-performing populations, though upper-level decision makers often do so without considering input from educators at the site level. Teachers inevitably become overwhelmed with the sheer number of new curriculums, technology, pedagogies, and assessments they are being asked to implement. Far too often, the outcome of this urgency to implement everything is that nothing gets implemented *well*. Instead, teachers just barely hang on as they muddle through the year, facing a learning curve that is entirely too steep. In contrast, leadership can limit focus to one or two initiatives with the input of educators. Then, collectively and systematically, they can implement and support resources such as materials, professional development, planning time, and collaborative data-analysis time that give both the initiative and the teachers required to implement the initiative more chances of being successful and avoiding initiative fatigue.

Derick's response to a negative school culture, feelings of isolation, and initiative fatigue was to start to feel burned out. Lessons became lectures, collaborative time turned into a rush to finish activities, and failure on benchmark assessments became the norm. Although this wasn't what Derick wanted for his students or himself, he just wasn't sure what to do or what to prioritize.

When I first sat down with Derick individually, I was a visiting PLC consultant and it was my third meeting in the school. I had been working with the school long enough to deduce that there was initiative fatigue building. This was not surprising to me. My first visit to the school two months earlier had been on a Friday afternoon. I learned as I left that I was the fourth consultant to visit that week and each of us represented a different initiative. Recognizing the position the school had put itself in concerning new initiatives, I knew my interactions with the staff needed to be calibrated to not only meet the intended goals related to PLC implementation, but I also had to be cognizant of how overwhelmed many of the educators were feeling and support them at this level as well. This meant keeping my finger on the pulse of what educators needed from me, including social-emotional support, as well as support with process and pedagogy. I was highly aware of this as I met with Derick.

My purpose that day was to go over the process of identifying essential standards for Derick's grade level. This is one of the PLC processes that allows educators to clearly identify and narrow down what they want their student to know and be able to do by the end of the academic year, by grade level or course. However, when I got to his classroom, I realized he was exhausted; his eyes and expression were glazed over. I surmised quickly that on this day, the last thing he wanted to do (or was even capable of doing) was to spend forty minutes with me to learn the process and criteria for identifying essential standards. On this day, Derick needed a lifeline. In this case, my job was to let him know it was OK to slow down, and to help him get in touch with his classroom and his purpose as the teacher. After sitting for a few minutes and listening to the panic in his voice as he discussed all he had to do, I assured Derick that it was OK if we didn't figure out essential standards today. Instead, we just talked. Through some probing questions, we were able to get down to some of the specific struggles that Derick was having. The most important for him was that he just didn't feel like he was connecting with his students. I knew from research and experience, this was a big one. I asked him for an example. He said, "Well, I spent all this time creating a scavenger hunt to spark interest in the math coordinates we were working on, and all I got was rolled eyes and minimal engagement." I had actually been in his classroom earlier and could see that this had not been a successful lesson. I asked him how it felt to be ignored and to feel disrespected through the noncompliance of his students. He told me honestly, "I hate it. I'm not even sure if I can do this anymore." *Ouch*. That was tough to hear. I felt for him, but I also couldn't just leave him there. I asked if we could explore some goal that might help him connect better with his students, and he agreed.

I began working with Derick to identify some personal goals using a goal-setting tool I will introduce here briefly and discuss more thoroughly in chapter 6 (page 97). My intent was to promote an ongoing practice of goal-setting that would connect his *why* as an educator to increased student outcomes. Based on our conversation, I directed him first toward Robert Marzano's "Teacher Scales for Reflective Practice" (2010). These scales identify research-based practices for teachers that, when implemented, have strong evidence for significantly impacting student learning. After we reviewed the scales together, Derick chose a goal from the section Lesson Segments Enacted on the Spot—Design Question #5: What will I do to engage students? (Marzano, 2010). Here's what he found under question number eight in that section, which asks the educator, "What do I typically do to provide opportunities for students to talk about themselves?" This question stopped him in his tracks. He confided in me, "I don't do this at all." I asked him why not, and he responded, "I don't know. I guess I was educated in schools where what the student thought wasn't that important. We were supposed to listen to the teacher, learn the material, then regurgitate it back on the test. I guess I just never thought about intentionally building in time to learn about what makes my students tick, what they really enjoy, or what they really fear. Maybe I'm even a little afraid to ask. What if they just blow me off?" I admired his brutal honesty and his willingness to take a deeper look at building connections with his students to improve learning outcomes. We looked at the scales (see figure 4.2, page 58) then began brainstorming some goals and identifying actions Derick could take to improve on involving students in their learning using the Autonomous Action Plan template (figure 4.3, pages 59–60).

Derick utilized goal setting, along with questions that allowed him to reflect deeply on his *why*, to identify steps he would take to meet his goal of bringing more student input and engagement into his classroom. He thought about how he would measure the outcomes of these steps and who would be his supporters and allies in the process. Because he was a singleton in his elementary school—the only teacher with the responsibility for fifth-grade standards—and did not have an established collaborative team, he identified others in his school that could offer ongoing support, like his instructional coach. He also identified the school's SMART goal that his individual goal would support. His thinking and process are represented in figure 4.3 (pages 59–60).

What do I typically do to provide opportunities for students to talk about themselves?	
The teacher provides students with opportunities to relate what is being addressed in class to their personal interests.	Notes

Teacher Evidence	Student Evidence
☐ Teacher is aware of student interests and makes connections between these interests and class content. ☐ Teacher structures activities that ask students to make connections between the content and their personal experience. ☐ When students are explaining how content relates to their personal interests, the teacher appears encouraging and interested.	☐ Students engage in activities that require them to make connections between their personal interests and the content. ☐ When asked, students explain how making connections between content and their personal interests engages them and helps them better understand the content.

How am I doing?

	Not Using (0)	Beginning (1)	Developing (2)	Applying (3)	Innovating (4)
Providing opportunities for students to talk about themselves	I should use the strategy but I don't.	I use the strategy incorrectly or with parts missing.	I give students opportunities to relate what is being addressed in class to their personal interests, but do so in somewhat of a mechanistic way.	I provide students with opportunities to relate what is being addressed in class to their personal interests and monitor the extent to which these activities enhance student engagement.	I adapt and create new strategies for unique student needs and situations.

Souce: Marzano, 2010.

FIGURE 4.2: Teacher scales for reflective practice.

*Visit **go.SolutionTree.com/leadership** to download a free reproducible version of this figure.*

AUTONOMOUS ACTION PLAN

SECTION ONE—The Action
Action and Steps: What is the action I (we) will take to address student learning needs based on current data?
I will implement strategies to increase student engagement based on research: <ul><li>Develop a protocol (survey) to learn my students' perspective on how often their interests and insights are taken into account when lessons are presented.</li><li>Identify and use a protocol that prompts me to spend time getting to know the interests and challenges of the students in my class (one-on-one interviews, group discussions, and so on).</li><li>Use student interests and experiences to build relevance into my teaching and classroom instructional strategies.</li></ul>
Rationale: What does the research say about this action?
When lessons are created with relevance for students in mind, and when students are given choice and input into how they are to engage in learning knowledge and skills, engagement increases. When engagement increases, learning outcomes increase. Marzano's meta-analysis of teacher practices indicate that educators who are able to connect with the personal interest of their students have better overall outcomes.
Collaborators: If you are collaborating on this action, who is your team and what common knowledge will be necessary for you to work collaboratively?
I am the only teacher in the 5th grade so I don't have a grade-level team. However, I asked my school instructional coach to work with me to reflect on the outcomes of my goals and to adapt my practices to increase student engagement.
SECTION TWO—SMART Goal
S—Specific—Who will this action impact and how?
Students in my class will demonstrate more engagement in classroom learning activities which will increase learning outcomes on math common formative assessments (and other subjects).
M—Measurable—What positive change in learning data do you intend to accomplish?
Increased student engagement in the classroom will be demonstrated by an increase in student outcomes on unit formative assessments on grade-level essential standards.
A—Attainable—How many students will this innovation impact?
The percentage of students scoring 85 percent or better on formative assessments will increase from 19 students to 25 students by the end of the third quarter.

FIGURE 4.3: Derick's goal-setting Autonomous Action Plan.   continued →

R—Results Oriented—How will you know if your action has made an impact? What is your data point?

Anecdotal records of engagement/increased student learning outcomes on common formative assessments and benchmark assessments will increase from 60 percent proficiency to 89 percent proficiency.

T—Time Bound—When will you (your team) evaluate your impact? With what tool?

I'm going to utilize the formative and summative assessments for each unit of instruction and the NWEA benchmark assessment given at the end of the third quarter.

What is your SMART Goal?

By implementing student engagement techniques in my classroom to increase student engagement in math lessons, the number of students who demonstrate proficiency on end-of-unit formative assessments on math essential standards, by scoring 85 percent or better, will increase from 60 percent (17 students) to 89 percent (25 students) by end of the third quarter.

SECTION THREE—My Posse

Who will be your champion(s) as you pursue this goal?

My principal and the instructional coach are aware of my goal and the intended outcomes. They have offered to provide support and guidance as I pursue ways to learn more about my students and bring more engagement into my classroom teaching and learning activities.

How will you celebrate this goal?

I will be sharing my progress and outcomes with my instructional coach and two other colleagues who teach math in third and fourth grades. They have promised to support my work and give input for suggested adaptations if necessary. I have also asked the principal if I can share my personal goal with my colleagues at our staff meeting to share how I used this adaptation in my teaching to impact student achievement.

SECTION FOUR—My *Why*—My Voice

How does this plan connect to your *why* as an educator? How does it highlight your voice?

I came into this profession because I wanted to make a difference in students' lives. I have found that instead of making a difference, I have been struggling to keep my head above water and keep the class engaged and discipline in order. My goal is by identifying student engagement in my teaching practice and following researched advice on how to connect and engage with my students, we will all be more successful and engaged in the learning process and there will be less discipline needs. I'll be better able to make that difference I entered the profession to make.

*Visit **go.SolutionTree.com/leadership** to download a free reproducible version of this figure.*

Derick's schoolwide goal, which identified increased student proficiency rates in both reading and mathematics on the state test, alone did very little to motivate his actions in the classroom. It was an important goal, but unfortunately not specific enough to be motivating. The school as a whole rarely revisited the goal, and it seemed related more to compliance on the school improvement plan than an intention for direct motivation. In fact, for Derick it created anxiety that he would not be able to meet the established goal. However, when he was able to connect his own growth as an educator to the needs of his students *and* to the collective schoolwide goal, things began to make sense. In his struggle to keep up with all the mandates he was required to fulfill as a teacher in a low-performing school, he had not taken the time to self-reflect, find his purpose, and use that sense of purpose to conceptualize and implement actions of value. He had not taken the time to identify what his students needed from him—or for that matter, what he needed from his students. As it turns out, they needed the same thing he did: an appreciation for their thoughts and ideas, some choice in meeting their goals, and to be heard and seen as individuals. Unfortunately, most of the initiatives in his school had failed to offer this insight. It had to come through the reflective practice that Derick initiated, which, in the long run, made the schoolwide goal make sense for Derick. By finding a way to connect personally to the schoolwide goal, he made huge gains in restoring his internal culture as an educator—his internal belief that he has the ability to impact learning outcomes for his students.

Derick's goal to give his students more voice in the classroom actually improved student behavior and academic outcomes. He found he really enjoyed his students as he learned more about their lives and provided more empathy and understanding about their struggles in school. This translated this into lesson plans that reflected student interests and built more authentic student engagement and collaboration into their learning. With this newfound connection with his students and the success he felt as a result of his intentional goal setting, he was able to more authentically engage in the practices of identifying essential standards, creating and evaluating data from formative assessments, and responding when students did or did not learn. His independent goal setting aligned and supported the schoolwide goal of increased proficiency rates in reading and mathematics. In fact, pass rates on common formative assessments in his classroom went from 60 percent to 85 percent for the third quarter. Derick had found a way to bring his voice and expertise back into the classroom. By setting and accomplishing simple goals that still allowed him to follow the school's initiatives, he began to rebuild his sense of himself as a powerful educator.

I share Derick's story because I want you to see that even though Derick was in a school that was mired in a do-as-you're-told culture, he still found the opportunity to find an area of importance that he had control over that would lead him to the goal of meeting his students' needs in the classroom and the schoolwide academic goals. And although he had no other fifth-grade teacher to collaborate with, he still engaged his learning community by reaching out to colleagues who would support him, give him feedback, and celebrate his efforts, enabling him to find success for his students while increasing his own sense of autonomy and competence in the knowledge that he could impact his students' learning.

Not only did Derick's actions have a positive impact on student achievement, they helped him feel less burned out and at odds with his students. The work Derick did independently and collectively with the colleagues with whom he engaged in the goal setting process is an example of work that *heals the internal culture of the educator.* Derick's goal setting and intentionality began the process of restoring his faith in himself as an educator—his sense of competence.

As Derick discovered, setting goals, taking action, finding support, and celebrating successes can bring new understanding of your power to create change. And with this newfound empowerment, you are equipped to more effectively use all of the educational literature, professional development, curriculum, technology, and program tools at your disposal, and create and build on your own tools of effectiveness as well.

If no one in leadership is guiding you toward the importance of using your autonomy to engage in action research to find effective ways to help your students, then you have to do it yourself. Don't wait. For Derick, students' engagement, brought about by having their voices heard and respected in an authentic way in the classroom, wasn't a schoolwide initiative. No one told him to do it. But Derick recognized that student engagement was a glaring deficit in his classroom and knew *he* needed to take action. By identifying what works for students in the classroom and targeting the goal that he knew was best for him and his students, he was able to make gains in student achievement that authentically supported the schoolwide goals and initiatives. His success also provided him with the evidence to positively influence others in his school community. Derick made his goal setting practice visible by asking his instructional coach and principal to follow him in the process. Because of this, he was later able to share his learning and experience with other educators in his school. By recognizing that he was not being successful in engaging students and then taking responsibility and positive action to reverse this pattern in his classroom, he was able to help other educators dealing with the same problems make similar changes in their practice. Success precipitates success!

So what does this mean for you? Even if you've been through the technical process of writing goals more than just a few times before, I ask you to revisit the practice of goal setting as a way to restore your belief that you can impact student outcomes in a significant way. I want you to start the process with what *you* know needs to change. Start the process knowing that you, as an individual or as part of a collaborative team, have or can find the insights and knowledge about which practices offer the greatest benefit for your students. In chapter 6 (page 97), I'm going to ask you to begin a goal-setting practice that will lead you to look deep to determine specific roadblocks, and then look deeper for the solutions that can bring the hope and success you envision. Using this process will put you on the path to creating more competence and self-efficacy in your work as an educator while impacting student achievement at the same time. Our next reflective practice will support this process.

Reflective Practice Through Goal Setting

What I would like you to do now is to start a goal-setting process with the intention of building competence while increasing student achievement. Go back and revisit reflective writing question number one (chapter 3, page 44). This question asked you to identify practices you have wanted to implement in your classroom, school, or district but have put off. I asked you to think about the intuitive insights that have come to you in the course of your practice as an educator—the insights that you feel could lead to positive changes that make a difference in student successes and achievement (not to mention your own!) if you were to act on them. I'm going to ask you to choose to move forward with at least one of those insights by setting a goal to make the intention a reality. You may choose to do this by setting an individual goal like Derick, or a collective goal that you and your collaborative team create together. Having a team to help flesh out your ideas and share in the journey can have important effects for all the students in your grade or subject area. Either way, the Autonomous Action Plan requires you to involve others in the process. If it's going to be a personal goal, you will identify those who will check in and be your champion on the path to meeting the goal. If embarking on a collaborative team goal, you will collectively complete the plan. By keeping this process collaborative, you ensure the need for relatedness as well as competence is supported. Both personal and team goals are powerful and essential if your primary intention is to ensure a continual rise in student achievement for all students in your school. For now, though, I want you to choose just one action, then set a goal, either with your team or independently, based on a strong intention for increasing student learning results and increasing your sense of competency in your practice. We'll create the goal now and then build out the action plan in chapter 6 (page 97).

Reflection—My SMART Goal

First, get your journal ready to use. You will create your own SMART goal, but not just yet. Before you begin writing, I want you to take a look at another example, and this time one that utilizes a collaborative team process from the start. The following three-step example is one I created to help you see how this process can work for you and your team. In this example, a teacher team begins with an action statement and ends with a SMART goal that will require collaborative work to implement.

1. The first step is articulating the action. In order to create the action statement, an educator or educators on the team must do introspective reflection work to discover something they would actually like to change or add to their current practice based on data. The following action statement is an example of what comes out of this introspective work.

    > I want to work with my grade-level colleagues to create a walk-to-learn program that ensures students with specific needs are grouped together and get targeted intervention based on our common formative assessment results.

2. The educators then brainstorm and articulate the specific outcomes they would like to accomplish by initiating the action using the SMART format as follows.

    > **S—(specific):** We want to increase the number of students who score 3 or better on the fourth-grade narrative writing rubric

on common formative writing assessments by utilizing small-group instruction to address learning gaps for students who score below 3.

M—(measurable): Currently only 70 percent of our students score 3 or above. We want 90 percent of our students to score 3 or above.

A—(attainable): We have evaluated the data and feel that with the extra support, at least 90 percent of our students can score 3 or above on the narrative writing rubric.

R—(results oriented): 90 percent of students will score a 3 or above.

T—(time bound): My team and I will measure success by utilizing the first-quarter writing assessment for narrative writing given in October.

3. Lastly, the team creates a SMART goal that focuses on their action statement and the intended outcomes in a SMART goal format.

> By implementing a walk-to-learn program in our fourth-grade schedule, we will use small-group instruction time to address specific student learning gaps in narrative writing (action). The number of students who demonstrate proficiency in grade-level narrative writing skills (specific) by scoring 3 or better on the fourth-grade narrative writing rubric (measurable) will increase by 20 percent (results oriented) from 70 percent to 90 percent (attainable) as measured on the first-quarter narrative writing assessment given in October (time bound).

Now, it's your turn. Write all of your own three steps to creating a SMART goal in your journal under the heading, SMART Goal. Choose one action from the list of possible actions you created for question one in the chapter 3 Reflection section (page 44) and write it as step one in your journal. Use the SMART format to articulate desired results for your action and label this as step two; you can do this yourself, or if you've chosen to engage your colleagues in your plan, do this with them. Finally, create a SMART goal that will drive your implementation and success, something you, or you and your team, can revisit frequently to stay motivated and on track. See figure 4.4.

> By _____ (your action), the number of students who demonstrate proficiency in _____ (specific skill) by scoring _____ (measurable) will increase by _____ percent (results oriented) from _____ percent to _____ percent (attainable) as measured on the _____ assessment given on the date of _____ (time bound).

FIGURE 4.4: Developing an action SMART goal.

*Visit **go.SolutionTree.com/leadership** to download a free reproducible version of this figure.*

Now, congratulate yourself on the creation of a solid SMART goal! We will talk more about the action plan format and steps needed to implement the action you have selected to meet this goal in chapter 6 (page 97). But for now, you have a strong SMART goal to keep you focused on the prize of more students meeting proficiency on grade-level standards. Good job!

5

Relatedness

The last of the three needs identified in SDT is *relatedness*. In this chapter, we explore what relatedness looks like in organizational teams and leadership. We look at research that demonstrates that the most productive teams in an organization support not only the attainment of the goals and objectives set forth but also the social and emotional health and well-being of its members as they work to attain those goals. We also look closely at how this dynamic plays out in the collaborative teams of a PLC.

What Relatedness Offers

Think of a time in your life when having a trusted group of friends around you helped you find a clear path and offered a great deal of comfort and support, particularly when faced with an important challenge or decision. A friend of mine, for instance, decided that finding a life partner was an important next step in his life. He had been in relationships in the past that were unsuccessful and, for a time, he thought he was better off alone. However, time helped him heal from his disappointments

In a professional learning community, educators create an environment that fosters cooperation, emotional support, and personal growth as they work together to achieve what they cannot accomplish alone.

—Richard DuFour, Rebecca DuFour, Robert Eaker, Thomas Many, and Mike Mattos and with some renewed clarity, he now felt sharing his life with a supportive and caring partner was what he truly wanted. After evaluating his busy life and his tendency toward being a homebody, he decided that the online dating scene was the best avenue to pursue. He created his profile and entered the world of online dating—but instead of just jumping in and hoping for the best, he asked close friends to be part of his *match posse*. Basically, he created a group of close friends whom he respected greatly and who understood his core values well enough that they could be an honest, supportive sounding board in this very important quest. So, as he met people online, he'd also share their profiles and information with his match posse. Sometimes they would all get a good laugh at the obvious mismatch presented, but ultimately, they helped my friend wade through the awkward process of putting himself into the dating scene. Having his match posse made him feel a little less vulnerable and the experience considerably more fun. I'm happy to share that the result of this collaboration was successful. My friend is now happily married to the person he found on online (and his match posse fell in love with him, too!).

The same kind of support my friend received when seeking to meet his personal goals and navigate one of life's more difficult journeys is valuable in professional life, too, as we move toward our aspirations and goals. In fact, identifying your *professional* posse is a critical and necessary part of your journey to heal your internal culture.

As with autonomy and competence, if relatedness is key to an overall sense of well-being and happiness, you will find that the PLC processes and culture are the pathway to the outcomes derived from relatedness, too.

I intentionally saved the need for relatedness for last. It was important that you first regained your understanding of how important autonomy is to your well-being and sense of empowerment. It was equally important for you to take that autonomy and identify actions and set goals that will support your success in securing your knowledge that you are competent and that your actions as an educator really can and do make a difference. It was also vital for you to understand that the fulfillment of the two critical needs of autonomy and competence lie in your hands—not those of some other person or group of people. So, regardless of the type of school or educational culture you find yourself in, you can embrace the power to take action and make the changes that support your well-being and effectiveness as an educator.

Consider now how relating to others in a collaborative team supports your need for autonomy and competence while providing the critical need we all have for relatedness. It is membership in a highly effective collaborative team that will not only heal the internal culture of the educator, but as a result begin the transformation of the culture in public education as well. As we nurture our own feelings of self-efficacy in our individual work as educators, and then carry this into our work with our colleagues, we are then ready to make an impact on education as a whole through our vision and empowerment to create and lead positive changes in public education.

What Is Relatedness?

Relatedness is described in psychological research as an innate need to establish relationships in which one feels close to others, cared for, and secure (Deci & Ryan, 2008). According to SDT, relatedness is a top indicator of happiness and well-being. Consider that, as educators, we spend over half our waking hours during a five-day workweek in the school or administrative office, a sense of relatedness with those with whom we spend this time is not only a good idea, it's critical. So why is it so often neglected?

If you've been in education for any length of time, you know that relating to your colleagues can land anywhere between two extremes on a continuum—lifesaving or energy-draining. In other words, you may have landed in a place where you feel safe in a collaborative team of educators who have a common vision of success and reinforce your sense of safety, belonging, and competence to meet your goals on the way to your vision. Or you may have landed at the other end of the continuum, as part of a dysfunctional group of educators who spend their time complaining about things they can't control, have become stagnant in their profession, or (the worst-case scenario) have turned against each other and essentially no longer communicate at all.

It's easy to see why many educators view relatedness in the work place as risky—maybe it will provide support and increased well-being, but maybe not. For some, bringing authentic relatedness into our schools and educational organizations can be seen as a double-edged sword. We have an innate desire to connect with others—to create and engage, to find support and belonging, to meet our goals collectively and with support—yet the exposure to the real or perceived vulnerability that connection represents can be unnerving. This is especially true if we have had unfavorable experiences in the past that have caused us to believe that the rewards of relatedness will not outweigh the potential hurt and frustration. So instead of facing hurt and frustration that *might* come with the vulnerability of connecting, many choose the alternative, which is some form of isolation—physical, psychological, or emotional.

I recently visited a department-level team in an attempt to facilitate collaboration around common data. This school was overwhelmed by low academic achievement and desperately needed to find common commitments to increase student outcomes and graduation rates. During this meeting, our purpose was to evaluate the results from a common formative assessment, determine the areas where students struggled, and then decide which supports and reteaching methods the team could implement to offer the best support for students who failed to demonstrate competency on the tested standard. To do this, we needed to answer some probing questions: "Which students did well and why? Which students were far from proficient and why? How will we collectively respond to support these students and on what learning targets should we place our focus?"

Although I tried to initiate the obvious conversations needed to answer these questions, the teachers were reluctant to engage. One teacher in particular was completely shut down. No eye contact, no engagement. Fortunately, I had built rapport with this teacher during prior visits and knew this was out of character. So, I finally looked at her and said, "What gives? Tell me what's going on." She chuckled at this, and then was gracious enough to explain, "I appreciate what you're trying to do, Robin, but this is not going to last. So, I'm not going to pretend. We never get the time or support to do the work of collaborating the way you've shown us. We never talk about what really matters. I'm just done trying to make it work."

Now, I don't know all the underlying frustrations that were going on inside my colleague that day, but this compulsion to shut down and just give up or go rogue can be very real. I do understand. It can happen when one feels unsupported, unheard, and out of touch with the collective vision and purpose of a team or organization. Shutting down can be a powerful urge when you've "had it!" However, you must resist this urge. Even though giving in may feel like a safer option, in the long run it only diminishes your power to impact the lives of your students and education as a whole. It causes you to isolate yourself when the foundational truth of relatedness in education is that educators need one another.

People generally choose isolation as a way to cope when the perceived danger (stress, overwhelm, failure, disregard) triggers the fight-or-flight response. If you are prone to flight as a coping response, you are more likely to choose some form of retreat. This may be demonstrated by an unwillingness to be a member of a group, or, if you must participate in a group, you become disengaged. Disengagement can show up physically, psychologically, or emotionally. When you regularly miss meetings or show up late, your disengagement is represented by a lack of physical presence in the group. It shows up psychologically when a member shows lack of engagement in the collective problem solving needed to determine how to increase success and competence. It shows up emotionally when a member shows a lack of passion about the group's vision, mission, goals, or collective commitments. Isolation or retreat can also happen when those who lean toward the fight response have spoken out vehemently against real or perceived injustices and failures in the system and have been met only with resistance and disregard. Like my colleague in the preceding story, when individuals feel unheard and disregarded, frustration can cause them to turn to some form of isolation.

Regardless of why one turns to isolation and what form it takes, all scenarios involving isolation are dangerous in our educational settings. Isolation eliminates the opportunity for the support and clarity that comes from working through roadblocks to find constructive ways to bring success to our work with students. Isolation is a stance that will never reap the rewards that a strong collaborative team can produce for both you and your students. More often than not, isolation exacerbates the feelings of fear and insecurity that you sought to isolate yourself from.

So how do we not only move past the tendency to isolate, but prevent it from occurring in the first place? To start, we have to shift our understanding of what elements of effective teams are most important and require our support. In his book *Effective Teamwork*, Michael West (2012) delineates the following two critical aspects of what healthy teams must focus on and support if the team is to be successful.

1. The task the team is required to carry out (their goals and objectives).
2. The social factors that determine how members work together as a social unit. These factors include the social, emotional, and other human needs (such as autonomy, competence, and relatedness) that are critical to the well-being of its members.

In the culture of public education, too often expectations are placed on educators in the area of task completion, yet the need for them to feel connected, cared for, and supported socially and emotionally in their quests to achieve those tasks is often neglected. This is where we go astray in our concept of effective teams in education. Our focus has become lopsided. We have a tendency to place all the emphasis on meeting goals while leaving to chance the social and emotional well-being of the individuals and teams charged to meet these goals—or we neglect this element altogether.

Five Indicators of Team Effectiveness

West's (2012) research identifies five indicators that bring members of a team closer to meeting both their goals and their individual and collective needs for connectedness and well-being. These indicators represent a focus on both the tasks associated with the goals a team aspires to accomplish (which is critical) and on the overall well-being of its members (also critical, but too often neglected). So let's look at the following five indicators of team effectiveness.

1. **Task-Related Objectives**—The degree to which the team is able to successfully meet their set objectives. In the school, this would be the collective and personal SMART goals that are developed to ensure all students are successful and learning at high levels.

2. **Team Member Well-Being**—The level of well-being members feel while accomplishing their work. This indicator could be characterized by low levels of stress, ability to ask for help when needed, high levels of trust, and high levels of satisfaction in their growth and successes, and correlates with competence.

3. **Team Viability**—The increased likelihood that the team will last and thrive as a highly effective team. This includes the degree to which they are compelled to continue their work together, to successfully support one another, and to meet common and individual goals.

4. **Team Innovation**—Innovation is the extent to which the team comes up with and creates new and improved processes, strategies, and systems to support their collective goals. This indicator correlates with autonomy—the freedom to act on the ideas and plans that provide innovation and challenge the status quo (the *loose* of the PLC).

5. **Inter-Team Cooperation**—This is a measure of how well the team works with other teams within the system. This indicator assesses the degree to which the teams create systems that perform well and respond to the needs of the organization as they arise (West, 2012).

Using these five indicators, West (2012) goes on to identify four potential types of teams that can be found in organizations: the dysfunctional team, the complacent team, the driven team, and the resilient team. These teams are defined by their ratio on a continuum of two potential characteristics: task reflexivity and social reflexivity. *Task reflexivity* is defined as a process whereby team members "actively focus upon their objectives, regularly reviewing ways of achieving, and the team's methods of working" (West, 2012, p. 7). Just as important is the *social reflexivity*, which is defined as a process whereby the team "reflects upon the way in which it provides support to members, how conflicts are resolved and what is the overall social and emotional climate of the team" (West, 2012, p. 7). It is these two factors—task completion and social and emotional well-being—coupled together that produce the highest performing teams. If we look at the four types of potential teams through the lens of educational teams, we can more effectively bring into focus the characteristics of a healthy school or administrative team that supports goal attainment and basic social and emotional needs for relatedness. See if you can recognize or identify with any of the characteristics listed in figure 5.1 (page 74).

TEAM EFFECTIVENESS	
High Task Reflexivity	
Type D: Driven team	*Type A: Resilient team*
• High short-term task effectiveness • Poor team member well-being • Short-term viability • Moderate innovation • High inter-team conflict	• High task effectiveness • Good team member well-being • Long-term viability • High innovation • High inter-team cooperation
Low Social Reflexivity	**High Social Reflexivity**
Type C: Dysfunctional team	*Type B: Complacent team*
• Poor task effectiveness • Poor team member well-being • Very low team viability • Low innovation • High inter-team conflict	• Poor task effectiveness • Average team member well-being • Short-term viability • Low innovation • Moderate inter-team conflict
Low Task Reflexivity	

Source: West, 2012.

FIGURE 5.1: Team effectiveness.

The Dysfunctional Team: Low Task Reflexivity With Low Social Reflexivity

The dysfunctional team may be thought of as the *assigned team*. Its members wouldn't be involved if they didn't have to be. They use the term *team*, but they are just groups of individuals with no norms or commitments to offering collective care and responsibility for their purpose or goals. Members have the potential to come across as aggressive in their communication or, on the other end of the continuum, completely disengaged in team discussions. Members go through the motions of working together, but in reality there are few positive outcomes, if any. In fact, members often resent having to meet at all. The tension in the room is often palpable, and apathy, resentment, or anxiety are the byproducts of the obligation to meet.

The Complacent Team: Low Task Reflexivity With Average Social Reflexivity

This team can be characterized as a group of educators who have become content with the status quo—whether it's a grade-level team, department team, or even a leadership team. Members get along relatively well but are not motivated to change the status quo, even when it has produced obvious shortfalls in student achievement. Over time, the complacent team's members have become numb to any sense of real passion about their calling to support and educate their students. Instead, they are content with just getting by. If they meet with any regularity, the meetings are usually socially motivated or take place because meeting is mandated by their principal or supervisor. They are not driven to set and monitor goals to achieve their collective purpose, nor are they motivated to support one another in meeting personal goals in their work as educators. If support is offered, it is often for the purpose of supporting the existing system to ensure it continues to run smoothly. This group may continue for a short period of time, but in the long run, members will generally seek to get out or move on.

The Driven Team: High Short-Term Task Reflexivity With Low Social Reflexivity

In this team, one or more members are driven to achieve, possibly due to a competitive nature. Other members either join in or get left behind. This team's members take their goals seriously and begin the process of determining steps to meet those goals quickly and efficiently. However, they may get stuck on system or process goals as opposed to achievement goals; they operate well in the beginning, but they don't necessarily achieve the results they were anticipating over the long run. The team may be moderately innovative, but only because one or two members do most of the talking; other voices are seldom heard. As a result, they are limited in their innovative success. Although this team is more likely to meet some of their short-term goals, the team's pace can leave members burned out and frazzled. As a result, these teams don't always last for the long haul.

The Resilient Team: High Task Reflexivity With High Social Reflexivity

This team of educators is in touch with their *why*. They know they have a calling to educate children and ensure each child has high levels of academic and social and emotional success. Their individual and collective goals, and their collaborative effort around these goals, ensure their success. This team has protocols to focus their work on the critical elements of student learning. They have developed collective norms that ensure the social and emotional well-being of the group's members are not neglected. Because they attend to both the task of ensuring high levels of student learning *and* the social and emotional needs of its members, they recognize when members of the team are feeling overwhelmed, which allows them to adapt timelines or share responsibilities to maintain a constructive pace but not at the expense of the emotional wellness of the team. This team has a high degree of cooperation, which allows them to quickly respond and innovate to ensure their goals are met, which in turn builds high levels of relational trust, ultimately ensuring the longevity of the group.

Now, the answer to the following question may be obvious, but I'm asking it anyway: "Which of these teams would you want to be a member of?" If you said the resilient team, good choice! Because this team, if consistently nurtured and maintained, not only will help restore the internal culture of the educator, it ultimately has the potential to restore the school culture and the culture of public education as well.

Resilience and the Collaborative Team in a PLC

As we explored earlier with autonomy and competence, the PLC model prescribes a form of collaboration represented in the resilient team. It is designed to support our innate needs for relatedness while also providing support to meet our collective and individual goals. In *Professional Learning Communities at Work*, authors Richard DuFour and Robert Eaker (1998) state clearly, "In a Professional Learning Community, educators create an environment that fosters cooperation, emotional support and personal growth as they work together to achieve what they cannot accomplish alone" (p. xii).

From its beginning, the PLC model of school improvement recognized the need for relatedness in the school setting. In creating a focused collaboration toward meeting your collective goals, you and your colleagues commit to the emotional support and personal growth of the educators within the community. This focused collaboration is a cornerstone of the PLC foundation. So let's explore how the systems, processes, and norms of collaborative teams in a PLC support relatedness and in turn support the internal culture of the educator.

In PLCs, educational structures prioritize grouping educators into collaborative teams that share common goals for student success. In a PLC, the collaborative team is established as the core of the work environment. The idea that you will have to work with and relate to your colleagues is inherent in the concepts of the PLC—the understanding that the only way to ensure all students learn at high levels is to work collaboratively. The importance of working together to improve our outcomes is a nonnegotiable. However, if we are to support both the goal attainment of the team and the social and emotional well-being of the team members called upon to meet these goals, we must be clear about our focus for each.

Let's start by looking at those areas that a collaborative team in a PLC focus on daily. I have listed some of the key characteristics and areas of focus for high-functioning collaborative teams in a PLC. I have discussed many of these through the course of this book, but let's look at them collectively.

High Functioning Collaborative Teams in a PLC: Key Areas of Focus

As we look in more detail at the following characteristics of PLC teams, see if you can find the correlation between the key areas of focus for high-functioning collaborative teams in a PLC (DuFour et al., 2016) and the five indicators of team effectiveness introduced earlier from West's (2012) research on effective teams (page 72).

- They have a clear and compelling purpose—a mission or a vision.
- They set SMART goals to monitor their progress toward this mission or vision.
- They require a mindset of collective responsibility for meeting those goals.
- They establish norms of behavior to ensure all voices are heard and mutual respect is nurtured as they support each other in the work of ensuring student learning.
- They have a clear focus and avoid burnout by limiting their focus to only those things guaranteed to bring about student success. The four critical questions of PLC teams ensure this focus:
    - ▸ What is it that we want our students to know and be able to do? (guaranteed and viable curriculum)

- How will we know if they have learned this?
  (common formative assessment)
- How will we respond when they don't learn to ensure that learning takes place?
  (multitiered systematic interventions)
- How will we respond when they do learn to ensure productive challenges are part of their experience?
  (multitiered systematic extensions)

• They participate in action research based on student data to adapt practices and ensure learning for all.

• They celebrate their successes collectively and often.

The succinct behaviors contained in the preceding list are very important. In fact, Jim Collins (2001), author of *Good to Great*, states that "The real path to greatness, it turns out, requires simplicity and diligence. . . . It demands each of us to focus on what is vital—and to eliminate all of the extraneous distractions" (Collins, 2001). This truth is what drives the idea of *tight* and *loose* in a PLC as we saw earlier in chapter 3 (page 35). The tight elements, the guiding principles of a PLC, and the focus of the collaborative teams within the PLC are what propel educators to greatness. The unwavering focus on these critical elements allows team members to move swiftly and determinedly in the direction of their vision to ensure all students are learning at high levels. So how do these key areas of focus in the collaborative team nurture relatedness and social and emotional well-being?

A Clear and Compelling Purpose

In a PLC collaborative team, identifying a clear and compelling purpose is the starting point. Team members take this process seriously and ensure that all voices are heard before moving forward. Just as I asked you to revisit your *why* at the beginning of this book, it is critically important for a resilient team to be clear on the collective *why*. The mistake teams of educators often make as they work together is to assume they all share a collective understanding of their mission or vision for their team despite never discussing and identifying it. In fact, when teams take time to clarify their mission and vision, they often find their assumptions are dead wrong. They discover that different team members have different answers if asked to define the mission and vision of the team. Unfortunately, teams generally don't ask!

Another aspect of a clear and compelling purpose is the school or team's collective values. When we consider West's (2012) work on social reflexivity, collective values become another important element that allows us to stay focused on our purpose while supporting the social and emotional well-being critical to effective teams. As we started implementing the turnaround model at our school, we not only identified our compelling purpose through our mission and vision, we also took time to identify our collective values.

Through a collaborative process, we clarified that our mission was to ensure that our students, who had been in a state of academic stagnation for years, must leave our school demonstrating grade-level proficiency on the Common Core standards. Our vision was to see our school become a school that transformed our expectations, pedagogy, and curriculum in such a way as to ensure high levels of learning for all. "Failure is not an option" became our mantra; however, even before we clarified and published our collective vision and mission statements, we clarified our collective values.

Bringing a diverse group of educators together for the first time—with half having gone through the trauma of the interview processes that would result in many of their colleagues being removed from their school—it was imperative that we paid close attention to the social-emotional side of our work together. There was a need to begin the process of creating relational trust, and we wanted to make this a priority. So we took an entire day to participate in team-building activities that concluded with a clarification of our collective values. To clarify our values, we worked through a process that started first with individual reflections on personal values. Then, by forming small groups that evolved into ever larger groups, we asked each grouping to narrow their values down to six to eight values that resonated with all the members. This required honest communication, personal reflection, and vulnerability—all aspects of building relational trust.

By the end of day, we had narrowed our individual values down to eight collective values that would drive our attitudes and norms toward each other and our school community as we moved forward. Each member of our staff committed to uphold the following values: respect, collaboration, honesty and integrity, dedication, open mindedness, positive attitude, and high expectations. It is my belief that this work on collective values was the beginning of the process that allowed us to let go of any confusion and hurt from the past and push toward the future to accomplish the mission and vision we all committed to achieving. The power of having collective values that relate to your clear and compelling purpose supports the social reflexivity that has shown to be a key influencer in highly effective teams.

Those teams that do not identify the *why* that drives them toward innovation and action research, as well as the values that support social-emotional well-being along the way, miss out on the passion and drive that lead to the innovations that challenge the status quo and increase learning for all. Beyond the importance of a collective focus, an important aspect of going through this process is the deeper form of trust and relatedness it requires as individuals talk openly about their personal values and goals, their collective purpose, and the collective commitments they are willing to make in their pursuit to ensure students learn. The process is powerful and must be done at the team level and the school level, so don't skip it. Make it visible and do it collectively.

SMART Goals

Ken Williams (2015), coauthor of *Starting a Movement*, has said, "You are not a team unless you have a goal that compels you to come together". I touch on both individual and team SMART goals in relation to the need for competence in chapter 4 (page 45). Now, I focus specifically on team goals that require teams to come together collectively to achieve those goals.

In *Learning by Doing* (DuFour et al., 2016), the *collaborative team* is defined as "teams of educators whose members work interdependently to achieve common goals for which they are mutually accountable" (p. 12). So again, don't skip this process. It is at the core of what makes a collaborative team a collaborative team. Create purposeful, attainable goals and ensure these goals come from a place of authenticity arising from your collective purpose and vision, not just from a compliance-based task. To quote Williams again, "Your goal must compel you to come together to meet this goal, you can't do it just for the sake of compliance" (Williams, 2014).

When teams take time to communicate honestly, identify where they want to go, and set goals to that end, they are participating in an authentic form of goal setting. When they achieve these goals, the outcome for the educators in that team is a higher level of connectedness, success and a strong sense of collective competence. And as we learned in chapter 4 (page 45), this outcome translates into a strong sense of well-being.

In addition to this collective competence, setting and attaining goals collectively also fosters a strong sense of relational trust. Sociologists Anthony Bryk and Barbara Schneider's (2002) work on relational trust in schools considers the feelings of competence that come from the interdependence of roles when attaining a collective goal to be one of the critical attributes of fostering relational trust. Relational trust is the foundation for the caring and connectedness inherent in relatedness.

One of the things I love most about my work as a coach and consultant in schools is that I get to watch teams of educators evolve over time. I recall one grade-level collaborative team I worked with that was struggling to build relational trust. If I had to categorize them, they would most likely fall into the complacent team category. They were all effective educators and seemed to get along well enough as a grade-level team. They worked collaboratively around school tasks such as establishing their duty schedule, helping with classroom materials, and volunteering for school events. Yet as I began to work with them, I realized they were quite uncomfortable participating in dialogue about formative data and student learning in their classrooms. They seemed reluctant to engage in the work of collaborating around student achievement and sharing best practices. They were content with just doing their own thing in the classroom and letting their colleagues do whatever it was that they did in their classrooms. They didn't have a collective goal or purpose that drove their actions and passion as a collaborative team of educators.

During my time with this school, the leadership team decided to create data walls in the grade-level hallways of the school. They created poster-size bar graphs that would serve to monitor the average quarterly results on the school's benchmark assessment. As the posters were hung with the baseline data bar highly visible on the bar graph, grade-level teams began setting goals for increased student achievement. This was the first time this grade-level team had participated in the SMART goal process. However, to my delight, they were agreeable to participating and began to create SMART goals each quarter based on the quarterly assessment outcomes. It was amazing to watch how this collective goal-setting practice galvanized this grade-level team around taking collective action. Suddenly, they had a shared purpose and goal for achieving that purpose. I watched joyfully and respectfully as the teachers began looking at their data and asking one another for ideas about how to more effectively teach certain standards and skills. They opened up to learning how to use certain processes like developing common formative assessments, utilizing data analysis protocols, and taking collective responsibility for the increased success for all of the students in their grade level by sharing students during intervention time. Their commitment to evaluate their current reality using data, create team goals to improve outcomes, and then work collaboratively to achieve their collective goals made all the difference for this team. They moved from being a group of educators who met regularly to a high-functioning team that was impacting student achievement.

During one of my last visits with this team at the end of the school year, I was invited to one of their celebrations. As I stood with them in the hallway, I looked at the bar graph on the wall that featured four bright blue bars with an upward trajectory of more and more students scoring proficient and above on benchmark assessments. Students sat cross-legged in the hall gazing up at their successes modeled by their bar graph and beamed with pride at what they, too, had accomplished collectively. It was a great time of celebration for students and for the members of the collaborative team. As I looked across at this powerful group of educators, I could see there was a new connectedness and trust between them that was not there when I first met with them at the beginning of the year. They had their arms around each other as they smiled broadly, reflecting what was no doubt a new sense of competence. They seemed to personify Bryk and Schneider's (2002) conclusions on relational trust that the feelings of competence that come from the interdependence of roles when attaining collective goals is indeed one of the most critical attributes of fostering relational trust and connectedness.

Collective Responsibility

In a collaborative team, you don't carry the responsibility for ensuring all students learn at high levels on your own. Members of high-functioning collaborative teams not only have a responsibility to ensure students are learning at high levels, they have a responsibility to one another to ensure they, too, are working and learning at high levels while supporting emotional and social well-being. This team ethos allows members to feel supported and safe in setting ambitious goals both individually and collectively to improve student outcomes.

During my tenure as an elementary school principal, the state passed legislation that mandated that 30 percent of a teacher's evaluation would be based on the state test scores and that teachers with high scores would be monetarily rewarded. Because the teachers at my school worked with students who came from high-poverty demographics, teachers and students were working diligently to close the achievement gap often present in low socioeconomic populations and were having great successes. Nonetheless, this unsettling news left them feeling panicked and, frankly, a bit demoralized. Teachers felt that using the state test to quantify their students' success, and their value as teachers, was unfair. I understood their concerns, yet I encouraged them to look at their situation from a different perspective. They were working in a school setting where collective responsibility was a value that was honored and cherished. Although the state policy-makers may not be looking at it this way, the teachers worked within a school culture that never pointed a finger at *your* kids—it was always *our* kids. This allowed teachers to reach out for help and collectively ensure academic successes for their students.

Because these teachers had a commitment to their values and norms, and felt a collective responsibility during their grade-level team meetings, there was already an embedded sense that if one team member was struggling to meet the academic or social-emotional needs of the students in his or her class, it was safe to share this with the team and get support. If data indicated that students were struggling to demonstrate proficiency on an essential standard, it became *our* responsibility to intervene, not *your* responsibility alone. I wanted these teachers to remember that we had already established a culture where educators support one another in their craft; when a student or a teacher is struggling, it is incumbent upon all to problem-solve to ensure high levels of learning and success.

Although the legislation as written was intended to work as an incentive by rewarding teachers with high test scores (which, as we saw earlier, has been proven by research to have little impact on either teacher motivation or student achievement), in a PLC, everyone is the hero, not just a chosen few. In fact, although the school improvement grant that supported the turnaround model also allocated money for rewarding individual teachers, the leadership team and staff decided to divide the money evenly between all fifty-two staff members, including ancillary staff members, such as instructional assistants and school secretaries. We knew our success was based on a collaborative team effort, and it is through the nature of this collective responsibility that authentic relatedness comes into the school or organization.

Norms for Communication and Mutual Respect

Just as we don't take on the responsibility for high levels of learning alone, neither do you have to take on communication and relational expectations alone. In PLC collaborative teams, we establish norms for our engagement and focus through a collective inquiry into what each member of the team values and what each needs to feel safe and communicate openly. Feelings of trust and respect can be nurtured when each person on the team has the opportunity to communicate his or her needs for safety and well-being in the context of the team's communications. Once established, these norms allow team members to stay on task and work through problems respectfully. Team members cherish their norms as they help the team adhere to its values. They remind team members that their agreements matter. When members disagree, they have protocols for coming to consensus. The team commits to hearing all voices and input, then moves forward collectively when the will of the group becomes evident. The group is not characterized by individual egos but by mutual respect for one another and the goals its members have set for student success. It's not that team members won't have disagreements; in fact, they value disagreements as the catalyst to growth. The group's common norms support its members' common respect, goals, and successes. Don't leave this to chance, because when norms are clear and respected, they create a team culture that nurtures relational trust.

I have found that different schools and even different teams within those schools may all have varied ways to establish norms and engage in critical conversations. Most norms are pretty easy for teams to identify and relatively easy to follow and agree on: be on time, focus on what we can change not what we can't, ensure all voices are heard, respect all opinions, follow through on agreements, stay focused on the four critical questions, and so on. However, there will be times when members of a collaborative team will have different ideas and opinions about how to move forward that are so disparate they challenge the trust and connection of the team. The communication that needs to take place during these times is referred to as *critical* or *crucial conversation*. These conversations are crucial because the health of the team is dependent on team members resolving differences. The way an organization or team handles these conversations is extremely important to maintaining trust and thus the internal culture of the educator. Team members must have an understanding of how they will handle these more critical conversations before emotional conflict emerges. One of the worst things a team or organization can do is ignore the problem and hope it will go away; however, if there is no established protocol for having these conversations, then this is often what happens.

There are many ideas and protocols for how to deal with conflict in organizations and teams. I encourage you and your staff or collaborative team to research ways of dealing with conflict together and agree on how you will approach critical conversations. However, let me share with you a list of suggestions from researchers (Kappel, 2017; Patterson, Grenny, McMillan, & Swizler, 2011).

1. **Embrace conflict:** As I mentioned previously, the last thing you and your team want to do is ignore a conflict that has the potential to fester and get worse. So get right in there and work through the conflict.

2. **Create the space:** Agree to create a time and place to talk about the conflict where you won't be interrupted and the team can honor the dialogue.

3. **Listen deeply:** Come to the conversation with an intent to learn about others' perspectives instead of defending your own point of view. This opens the door to understanding and resolution.

4. **Come with compassion:** Conflicts are hard on everyone. Having an open heart and a willingness to understand other points of view as much as your own is very important.

5. **Find common ground:** As part of a team that shares common goals and desires for student achievement, seek to find the areas you agree on and build on these common understandings.

6. **Agree on how you will move forward:** Determine what actions you will take to ensure you and your team can move forward collectively.

7. **Be quick to forgive:** Apologize when appropriate, forgive when needed, and be grateful that you have had the opportunity to find common ground.

A Clear Focus

Under the construct of collective commitments, PLC collaborative teams have a clear focus when they meet together: the four critical questions of a PLC. First, they focus on what they have collectively decided all students must learn—the guaranteed and viable curriculum. Next, they determine collectively the common formative assessments needed to determine if students have learned the standards identified as essential to their growth and progress in school and in life. Based on the results of their assessment, they work collaboratively and collectively to identify what students need to learn and then set up systems of interventions and extensions that ensure all students receive the support they need. This process is hugely edifying. It brings teachers together to share ideas, think creatively, and support one another in responding effectively to student needs. You don't have to go it alone. Educators in a PLC have a clear focus and intimate knowledge about all the students represented by their team and the collective and individual goals of its members.

Celebrating Our Successes

Celebrating what we have accomplished in any area of life is extremely rewarding and adds to our happiness and well-being. All of us can think of times when we were celebrated or rewarded. The celebration and reward could have been for an individual accomplishment like running a marathon, earning first chair in the orchestra, receiving a college degree, or winning the blue ribbon at the art fair. The celebration could have been a collective recognition, like being a member of a team that takes the overall prize or award. We need opportunities to celebrate successes in our work as educators as well.

In education, districts and schools are recognized in a very public manner at times. For example, the federal government, state, or district often gives awards to schools for accomplishments in student achievement outcomes such as the Blue Ribbon School award given by the federal government. However important this public recognition seems, the celebrations that happen between you, your colleagues, your school, or your department often have the biggest impact on our day-to-day satisfaction and well-being. So I encourage you to take time to share your own personal victories, such as Derick's success engaging with his students that I describe in chapter 4 (page 54). Share your collaborative team victories with your school at staff meetings and assemblies. It is these often unseen, cumulative victories and celebrations that propel us onto the stage of larger victories and celebrations. So start with the small wins. Track them and make them visible. This is where we begin to find our joy and motivation in our work as educators.

Shared Leadership—Adding Another Lens

Before ending the discussion of relatedness, I want to touch on the idea of *shared leadership* in the context of collaborative teams and our need for relatedness. When we think of leadership, we often think about the person at the top—the person with the title. If you try to find a definition of leadership online, you'll find there are as many concepts and ideas about the true definition of leadership as there are websites focused on leadership. Wherever you land when choosing a definition of leadership, as educators we can agree that school and district leadership represents the person or people charged with leading and supporting the school or organization toward its intended vision and outcomes.

In education, the *leader* is often considered to be the superintendent, the principal, the head learner, or whoever holds any other title that bears the responsibility for leading the members of the school or organization. And these leaders are without question critical to this pursuit. Educational author and researcher Michael Fullan (2014) has written extensively about the importance and power of the principal. In his book, *The Principal: Three Keys to Maximizing Impact*, Fullan brings into focus one of the key concepts I have discussed throughout this book: the need for educational leaders to effectively manage the continuum between the disempowering practices of mandated program fidelity and the chaos that can come from educators who want to do their own thing without considering the collective commitments of the school. While the principal or educational leader in a school is vital to leading the necessary changes that increase student learning and success, shared leadership in a school is equally important and necessary.

In a PLC, shared leadership is highly valued and critical to success. It calls on educators to relate to one another as they strive to meet their collective goals and commitments. Shared leadership brings collaboration and relatedness into the realm of leadership instead of maintaining a top-down model of decision making that isolates members of the learning community. A go-it-alone leadership style can produce the same problems of isolation and ineffectiveness that educators encounter when collaboration is not prioritized. The concept of shared leadership is just that: sharing the responsibilities of leadership necessary to influence what Dufour et al. (2016) describe as a "complex change process" (p. 27). In a PLC, when we think of shared leadership, we generally think of the *guiding coalition*, or what some schools may call the leadership team. The guiding coalition alone, however, does not capture the totality of shared leadership. Collaborative teams are also part of the shared leadership within the school. But first, let's start with the guiding coalition.

The Guiding Coalition

The guiding coalition, or leadership team, is made up of members chosen for their ability to bring different leadership talents to the table to accomplish the schoolwide goals, while supporting one another along the path to meeting these goals. Shared leadership is birthed out of the second big idea of a PLC: working in collaborative teams with collective commitments. Just as no one teacher can meet the needs of all students, no one leader can meet the needs of all the members of the school community, and just as teachers cannot attain the vision and mission of high achievement for all without working collectively, neither can leadership. To successfully create lasting change, the responsibility of leading that change must be shared. In *Learning by Doing*, DuFour et al. (2016) state this point clearly:

> Those who hope to lead the PLC process must begin by acknowledging that no one person will have the energy, expertise, and influence to lead a complex change process until it becomes anchored in the organization's culture without first gaining the support of key staff members. (p. 27)

Those "key staff members" form the guiding coalition. In Ken Williams and Tom Hierck's (2015) book, *Starting a Movement*, they define the *function* of the guiding coalition as "creating and sustaining a culture of collective responsibility" with the *purpose* to "unite and coordinate the school's collective efforts across grade levels, departments, and subjects" (p.18). Generally speaking, members of the guiding coalition are representatives from the different grade level, subject area, or department-level teams. There will also be representatives from other support areas such as the counselor, special education department, ancillary staff, and instructional coach, if the school has one. When members on the guiding coalition represent the different areas of the school, the shared understandings and actions are more effectively implemented "across grade levels, departments, and subject areas" (Williams & Hierck, 2015, p. 18).

You most likely have a leadership team at your own school. But the truth is, being on a guiding coalition in a PLC is a different kind of commitment. As Williams and Hierck (2015) point out, one of the shifts that must happen in a PLC guiding coalition is a shift from messenger to missionary (p. 23). Why is this? Let's look at an assertion from Richard DuFour, Rebecca DuFour, and Robert Eaker (2008) in *Revisiting Professional Learning Communities at Work*, where they define a *guiding coalition* as "An alliance of key members of an organization who are specifically charged to lead a change process through the *predictable turmoil* [emphasis added]. Members of the alliance should have shared objectives and high levels of *trust* [emphasis added]" (p. 467). This assertion highlights once again the importance of relational trust and explains why educators must make the shift from messenger to missionary, which is not always easy. In many leadership-team scenarios, a teacher decides to sit on the team because he or she is next in line or drew the shortest straw, or the team voted him or her in. But if you have a mission to ensure members of your team are actively engaged in the collective commitments identified by your school in pursuit of *its* mission, then your work on a leadership team becomes different. It becomes more than just communicating information that is given to you to recite back to others. Instead, you must become the passionate cheerleader guiding and supporting your collaborative team toward agreed upon commitments and actions that will bring to fruition your collective vision—hence the term *guiding coalition*. Understand that, inevitably, those schools that have the most success creating change that impacts student achievement are those schools where the administration has prioritized its work with the guiding coalition. The coalition members meet regularly to evaluate and strengthen their schoolwide systems to ensure they support teachers and students to achieve high levels of learning. They take their leadership roles seriously and execute their responsibilities with passion.

Now that we've hit on the importance of the guiding coalition and its critical role in shared leadership, let's talk about the collaborative team's role. Often, teachers get stuck seeing *shared leadership* as a function of the guiding coalition alone. What you can't forget is that in a PLC, shared leadership refers to *all* members of the learning community. Inherent in the definition of a leader is the expectation that the leader, or leaders of the organization, will guide team members such that the team members focus on learning from their leaders. And in a PLC, that leadership is the responsibility of all members. If action research is at the heart of what team members do in a PLC, and if you are all working to improve your practice to impact student outcomes, then you will no doubt begin discovering and utilizing practices that have high-leverage yields for your students. When these high-yield practices begin to show results, team members must not only take responsibility to learn from colleagues who have demonstrated the successes, the team as a whole must learn from successful collaborative teams as well. This focus on the collaborative team as leading and educating is important, and I don't want you to miss it. Team dynamics and functioning are learned skills that must be developed in all members of a collaborative community, if you want your efforts to be successful. If there is a team whose dynamics and functioning are going well, other teams must be willing to learn from that team, and that team has to get comfortable sharing their experience in getting to that point. This is the power and purpose of the PLC!

So now I will bring into clearer focus the last of West's (2012) resilient team indicators, which is inter-team cooperation. Again, West describes this indicator as the measure of how well the team works with other teams within the organization and the degree to which it creates high-performing systems able to respond to the needs of the organization as they arise. Let's look at how educators can support shared leadership through the lens of the collaborative team.

Collaborative Teams

One of the primary trends occurring in education at the time the PLC model entered the educational conversation is called the *silo effect*. It describes a situation in which teachers find themselves isolated in their classrooms, rarely collaborating with their colleagues to meet student needs or identify best practices to meet those needs. The good news is that we've come a long way in setting up the systems that allow teachers to share best practices teacher to teacher. Not only have districts and schools become more aware of the need for educators to work collaboratively, they also are building collaborative time into school and district schedules with greater frequency and consistency. The widespread visibility of and experience with DuFour and Eaker's vision of Professional Learning Communities at Work and its verified success in schools and districts throughout North America is largely responsible for this change.

Yet while we've come a long way in breaking down the silo effect for teachers within teams, I want to also focus on how learning happens team to team. When I observe and talk to principals about their school's collaborative teams, they often reflect on how one or more teams are really moving forward, celebrating successes, and generally feeling great about their work. Yet, other teams in the same school struggle with lack of commitment to common goals and actions and have difficulty working collectively. If you work in a school that supports collaborative teacher teams, you've probably seen this yourself. It happens more often than we like to acknowledge. At the same time that something really powerful is taking shape in one grade level, department, or subject area team, other teams in the same organization may be genuinely struggling, and too often, the burden for supporting these teams falls solely on the principal, or possibly the instructional coach. This is where shared leadership in relation to team-to-team leadership comes in.

The school and learning community must move from simply noticing struggling teams to doing something constructive to support these teams at the inter-team level and ensure the struggling team is not isolated. In reality, struggling teams exist within a community where there are also high-functioning, resilient teams working together productively and successfully. If the high-functioning teams are not working to support the struggling teams, they're missing a big part of shared leadership. In a PLC, teachers in collaborative teams expect to support the teachers who are struggling within their team—and they should also expect that their teams will support other teams within the school community. Yet, too often teams do not share their practices of support outside their collaborative teams. Instead, collaborative teams struggle independently, just as individual teachers did before the idea of collaboration became part of the educational culture.

Collaborative teams that do not focus on intentionally sharing their practices across the organization contribute to team isolation. Whether your team is high functioning or struggling doesn't matter; isolation is bad for either one. When team isolation becomes the norm, this promotes division instead of development of more collaboration and relational trust throughout the school. Unchecked team isolation can result in a sense of tribalism, where members of the team find safety in their own collaborative team but never build that same relational trust and collaboration between teams. This can lead to exclusion that potentially turns into envy or even resentment among teams and in the culture of the school as a whole.

Here's the good news: the silo effect in collaborative teams within a school or organization can be easily remedied by bringing it into focus and creating pathways for teachers and department teams to collaborate more frequently and effectively. Through shared leadership, schools and educators can create the schedules, protocols, and expectations for teams to collaborate with other teams in the building. The same process that works in collaborative teams will work with inter-team collaboration. Intentional systems and protocols that foster the same collaboration between teacher teams as that which occurs between individual teachers is the only way to help relatedness and relational trust grow throughout the school. No magic wand bestows relational trust on a person or team; it only comes through taking the risk to reach out and grow and learn from one another, which is undoubtedly why inter-team collaboration is identified as one of the key indicators of resilient, high-functioning teams.

I have witnessed positive results in schools that intentionally create systems that ensure team-to-team collaboration. In a secondary setting, principals create staff meetings with the sole purpose of making time for department-level teams to share their best practices with other department-level teams. In one school, the principal became aware that the science department team was struggling to develop a system of data collection that allowed them to analyze formative assessments in such a way that members could easily assess and implement targeted interventions for individual learning targets. Knowing that the mathematics department had successfully created a system of data collection that allowed them to do this effectively, the principal made it a priority to make time for these two teams to work collectively to build a data system for the science department that could match the effectiveness of the mathematics department's system.

In addition, I've watched an elementary principal use professional development money to provide grade-level teams with extended time after school or during a professional development day to share best practices and create alignment of standards. One sixth-grade team that developed a system for creating flexible groupings based on learning targets received time to help the third-grade team develop similar protocols that allowed them to efficiently grade common formative assessments, place students in the appropriate intervention groups, and monitor progress toward proficiency to ensure group flexibility and movement.

Both of these scenarios allowed department- and grade-level teams to learn from one another and improve their practices using data to act quickly to respond to student needs. Instead of feeling isolated from one another, the members of these teams now had the experience of learning from one another in a collegial, nonthreatening, and supportive way. Even in schools where teacher isolation has been eradicated, these intentional efforts to ensure inter-team communication and collaboration break through another limiting barrier: collaborative team isolation.

I focus on this aspect of shared leadership because the collaborative exchange between teams, just as between teachers, is crucial to expanding our relatedness and sense of safety and well-being in our schools. With this in mind, I challenge you to evaluate the ways your school or district promotes or neglects collaboration and relationship-building among teams, particularly if you are a school leader or sit on a guiding coalition. In order to successfully duplicate best practices throughout the school, it takes all members working to increase collaboration and thus relational trust and relatedness. With focus, intention, and a little bit of planning, educators, the school administration, and the guiding coalition can all work together to set up consistent and effective systems and avenues for the collaborative teams to share and learn from one another across departments and across grade levels. We will look more closely at how you can support this practice in your own school in our reflective writing at the end of this chapter. Now let's look at one more advantage of fostering relatedness in our school communities to bring about an increased sense of fulfillment.

Finding Your Flow

In Mihaley Csikszentmahalyi's body of work on finding your flow, he discusses the importance of working collaboratively to find one's flow and revive one's passion in life. According to Csikszentmahalyi's (1990) research, *flow* is described as "a state in which people are so involved in an activity that nothing else seems to matter; the experience is so enjoyable that people will continue to do it…for the sheer sake of doing it" (p. 4). When was the last time you felt that way about your work as an educator? This phenomenon of flow is about happiness and well-being. We've all experienced this feeling when we've been so engaged and engrossed in what we are doing, time just slips by. It's an empowering feeling that displaces apathy and boredom and compels us to move forward.

Relatedness in all areas of the learning community brings us closer to finding our flow. Working with a group of individuals to promote the achievement of collective and individual goals increases the potential for the state of well-being that comes with flow or being *in the zone*.

> A successful interaction involves finding some compatibility between our goals and those of the other person or persons, and becoming willing to invest attention in the other person's goals. When these conditions are met, it is possible to experience the flow that comes from optimum interaction. (Csikszentmihalyi, 1997, p. 5)

I love this idea of "optimum interaction." Working collaboratively and supporting one another toward attaining successes for your students is one of the most rewarding aspects of education, found most readily in collaborative teams with a clear focus for creating successes for their students. Consistent growth and success occur when a person feels an internally motivated desire and conviction to support his or her team based on a commitment to not only the task but the well-being of team members. Real change happens when you are internally motivated toward relatedness and toward success in meeting your stated goals.

Reflection

At this point I hope you're convinced that educators absolutely need one another to restore their internal cultures and impact the greater school culture and culture of public education. Effectively communicating and relating with one another around common goals with mutual respect and support is the difference between mundane meetings and powerful, motivating collaboration. Please stop now and reflect on some of the ideas presented in this chapter with the goal of identifying your current reality and then create some of the actions you can take to initiate, fine-tune, or heal the painful experiences that contribute to your current situation and perspective regarding relatedness in your educational setting.

1. Based on the research covered thus far, what are you currently feeling about the need for relatedness to improve your well-being as an educator? Has the research caused you to reflect on your own level of collaboration and relatedness in your school or educational setting? Has the level of collaboration you've engaged in caused you to feel a sense of connection with and care for your colleagues or has it caused you to realize it's lacking for you?

2. Are you currently a member of a team in your school or district setting? Who are the members of this team? List their names. If you are not currently a member of a team in your school or program, reflect in your journal on why you're not. Is there an opportunity that you may not have considered to work with specific colleagues to form a team to achieve common goals? If so, list the colleagues' names. How could you reach out to these individuals?

3. West's (2012) research on effective teams identifies four types of teams based on their effectiveness in task and social reflexivity. Go back to pages 74–76 and take another look at the characteristics that describe each team in an educational setting. Which one comes closest to describing your team as it is right now?

4. Now go back and look at the descriptions of the five indicators of team effectiveness earlier in the chapter (pages 72–73) as they relate to

both task completion and the social and emotional support and well-being of its members. How would you rate your current team, school, or department on each of these indicators on a scale of 1–5, 1 being not important to my team and 5 indicating this is a high priority for my team?

- Task-related objectives   1   2   3   4   5
- Team member well-being   1   2   3   4   5
- Team viability   1   2   3   4   5
- Team innovation   1   2   3   4   5
- Inter-team cooperation   1   2   3   4   5

5. Considering your answers to questions 3 and 4 in this exercise, what do you, or you and your team, need to do to create a more effective collaborative team in the area of task or goal attainment? What do you or your team need to do in the area of social and emotional well-being or relatedness? Write down your ideas in your journal.

6. What first steps will you take to begin the process of creating a more effective team? What first steps can you take independently and what first steps must you take collaboratively? List them and attach timelines. Your steps represent your first goals on the path to improving the conditions of relatedness and social and emotional well-being in your workplace as an educator. Congratulations!

7. Finally, consider how collaborative teams can more effectively support one another in school communities to form a more authentic inter-team collaborative culture. What factors (lack of safety, competition, time, and so on) in your school, or in your experience, inadvertently or intentionally support collaborative team isolation?

8. Considering the factors you identified in question 7, what systems or norms could be established in your school or district to break down some of the barriers to inter-team collaboration (such as biweekly or monthly cross-team collaboration time, collaborative team mentor groups, and so on)?

6

Finding Your Voice

I felt compelled to begin writing this book by the pervasive sense of powerlessness expressed to me by so many teachers and administrators I have spoken with during my work with schools. I can't count the number of times I have heard teachers or administrators literally or metaphorically throw up their hands and lament that they have no power to make changes, even if they realize changes are necessary. For a variety of reasons, they think themselves powerless to change obvious flaws in the systems and protocols in their schools and districts that potentially allow hundreds of students to slip through the cracks and underachieve each year. The flaws could be present in many places: the curriculum, the scheduling, the assessment protocols, or students' ability to obtain interventions and extensions without losing access to core grade-level instruction. When faced with barriers to the changes needed, the refrain was the same: "What can I do? I don't have any control over these things." Teachers see the need for change and want to initiate, but believe they have no power to do so. This all-too-pervasive belief system—that one has no power to change things for the better in

It took me quite a long time to develop a voice. And now that I have it, I am not going to be silent.

—Madeleine K. Albright

education—is disturbing. Yet I fear this is what the culture of public education too often teaches educators. It tells teachers to be compliant, do as they're told, and everything will be all right. But everything isn't all right!

Educators have become resigned to a fate that says they no longer have any significant power or influence, no longer have a voice in what goes on to improve student learning. If there is any message I want you to take with you after reading this book, it is that you absolutely do have power! You may have lost sight of your power, but it is by no means gone. Our voices are our power, and we must find them again if we are to change the current trajectory of public education.

Finding Your Voice and Sharing It

The purpose of restoring the internal culture of the educator—those internal beliefs about your ability to make a difference in the lives of your students—is to begin the process of impacting not just your own experience as an educator, but the experiences of all educators within your sphere of influence. Yes, you cannot change systemic flaws overnight, but change starts when groups of empowered educators who have reclaimed their autonomy and sense of competence bring that empowerment into their larger sphere of influence. You must find your voice and step up to the plate and share it, share your talents and passions in the context of relatedness with your colleagues. When you take that step, collective empowerment, vision, and sense of mission begin to change the culture of public education.

Stephen Covey (1989), author of *The 7 Habits of Highly Effective People*, was a pioneering thought leader on how to effectively implement change and find success in both one's professional life and one's personal life. In fact, for almost thirty years his book has been changing the way people approach their careers and lives. Nonetheless, almost fifteen years after the publication of this groundbreaking book, he wrote another book adding one more habit to his seminal work. The book he wrote is called *The 8th Habit: From Effectiveness to Greatness*. So, what is this eighth habit that is so important that Covey wrote an entire book on it? You guessed it—finding your voice. What follows is how Covey defines *voice*.

> When you engage in work that taps your talent and fuels your passion—that rises out of a great need in the world that you feel drawn by conscience to meet—therein lies your voice, your calling, your soul's code. (Covey, 2004, p. 5)

Finding your voice isn't just about speaking up. It means being clear about your talents, your passions, and your purpose. It also means being clear about the direction you want your life to take, your career to take, then engaging in actions to influence your environment toward creating this future. Finding your voice means not only digging deep into your purpose and unique talents, but embracing them as your unique gifts, then using them to take action to start creating a reality that matches your passion and vision. Exciting, right?

With this understanding of voice in mind, let's revisit the *why* statement I asked you to create at the end of chapter 2 (page 33). Is there anything you want to add or adapt? Take a moment to reflect on it now and rewrite it if you need to. When you are finished, write it in your journal or in the following space available in the book.

I choose to be an educator at this time in my life, at this time in history, because . . .

_____

_____

_____

Now reread what you wrote a few times. Let it sink in. How well does your statement resonate with your purpose in education? What changes do you want to make in your career to ensure your *why* is on track? Take a moment to reflect on this in your journal.

I revisited my *why* recently when I moved to a different state and left the school district in which I had taught and been a principal for over fifteen years. I had completed my fifth year acting as the principal of the school I led through the turnaround model, and I had a strong sense that it was time for me to move on. My assistant principal who was at my side as we initiated the turnaround model was primed to take over, and I was ready to pursue new goals for my professional life, as well as my personal life. After leaving, I struggled to find my way at first. I thought I would just pick up the mantle of principalship again in a highly competitive new district and be on my way, but no positions opened up in this district. In fact, doors were being closed consistently, and I began to doubt my value and direction as an educator. After some deep soul-searching and failed attempts at recreating myself in a different field altogether, I was compelled to revisit my *why* as a person and as an educator. Through this process, I discovered a strong sense that my purpose now was to impact a larger body of educators. I wanted to become a catalyst to help schools begin the process of transforming their school cultures, begin solidifying their collective missions and visions, and begin creating the collective commitments that would allow collaborative work to ensure all students have the opportunities for high levels of success in school and in life, regardless of socioeconomic status. It was this sense of purpose that pointed me in the direction of becoming a consultant to help educators initiate the processes and systems to become high-functioning PLCs and experience some of the successes I had in my own school.

At first, I wasn't certain of my ability to share my voice—I doubted I had the influence necessary to facilitate the change I hoped to bring to schools. I didn't get it all right at first. But by trusting in my *why*, my vision for what I wanted to offer public education, I was able to trust my intuitive knowledge enough to take action. I had to take a leap of faith and go into schools, initiate the conversation, and begin the work of building relationships and creating change. That first step of courage to put myself out there helped me find my voice, begin fulfilling my purpose, and begin facilitating positive changes in schools. Knowing, following, and giving voice to my *why* and my purpose has brought me great fulfillment.

I share my experience to say this: it can be scary to put your voice into the conversation. What if I'm not as talented as I think I am? What if my idea is not successful? What if I get shut down? What if I fail? What if I just don't feel like I have the energy to do it? These fears are all valid concerns, and they doubtless come up for you at times. However, I ask that you trust your *why*—your purpose—and dig deep to find your innate courage. Push through the fear and take action even when it feels like you can't or have lost your motivation. Because the truth is, you must. Actions that bring you closer to your purpose, your *why*, your flow, your truth—it is these actions that restore drive and your energy for the work that you do in education. Even if the action you take is not perfect, it moves you out of your current reality and toward a vision of education that feeds your passion and ultimately makes the difference in the lives of your students and colleagues. By taking action, you (1) make a choice, (2) act on that choice, and (3) move closer to your purpose by meeting the goals you've set along the way. By taking autonomous action—an action that you, or you and your collaborative team, choose and have control over—you've moved out of a victim mindset and into an empowerment mindset. So let's start taking some action!

Now, let's explore how to get your voice back into the arena of school reform. I've talked about how to begin healing your internal culture by regaining your power through autonomy, competence, and relatedness. Now you can take steps to use that empowerment to bring out your authentic voice—in your classroom, in your team, in your school, in your district, and in the arena of public education. Taking such steps requires a clear understanding of what motivates you, a clear plan of action, and, most important, courage. So dig deep. If you were not meant to be a change maker in education, you wouldn't still be reading this book.

First Things First: Letting Go of the Past

Your journey began with reflecting on times in your educational career when you felt powerless. I asked you to remember the specific times and events that caused you to feel this way, then to take a moment to recall how that powerlessness felt and how it impacted you in your career. Recall that I asked you to put those memories aside and come back to them later. The time has come to revisit those moments. Go back to your reflection at the end of chapter 1 (page 20). Revisit one or more instances in your career when you felt powerless and how that powerlessness felt to you as an educator.

Perhaps these memories still bring up some pretty unpleasant emotions. I ask that you acknowledge them one more time. Recognize the injustices they represent to you. Then let them go. The only way you can be fully empowered to lead the change that will bring joy and fulfillment back to your career in education is to let go of the resentments of the past. A close friend and mentor once told me that there is no such thing as justified anger. I remember dismissing this idea when I first heard it. I said to myself, "Isn't it our anger that allows us to fight against injustices?" Personally, I have come to learn through life experiences that anger generally just robs us of the ability to effectively bring about positive changes in the circumstance that caused the anger in the first place. Don't get me wrong. I don't have a magic wand that will instantly allow you to let go of any resentments you may be carrying around with you. Letting go can be hard work. But I encourage you to work through any resentments you may be carrying. Maybe you will remember Pennebaker's (1991, 1997, 2004) research on journaling that I shared in the introduction of this book. His research indicated that those who greatly benefit from journaling about difficult experiences are those who used the writing experience to let go, disengage, reframe, and move forward from their disappointments or challenges. How you do this is really for you to discover. Some people just choose to forgive; some resolve not to let thoughts about negative experiences steal peace of mind any longer; others learn to accept that individuals who have dismissed or offended them were just doing what they thought was right at the time. No matter how you choose to let go, I encourage you to begin changing your mindset to one of moving forward rather than remaining mired in the past. There is nothing any of us can do to change what has happened in the past, but there is a lot we can do to change what will happen in the future.

I ask you now to journal about how you will begin to let go of your resentments related to your work in public education. I hope that you're ready to write it down and let it go, but if not, that's OK, too. However close or far you may be from letting go, take a moment to write down your thoughts and feelings about releasing any resentments you have regarding your experiences in education. This is a practice of clearing out—both mentally and emotionally—that creates room to create and act on a new plan to usher in hope and empowerment.

Autonomous Action Plan

Before I move on, I ask that you access the Autonomous Action Plan tool I presented in chapter 4 (page 59). I have created a blank template which you can download at **go.SolutionTree.com/leadership**. Or, review the copy printed at the end of this chapter (pages 112–114). I have given it this title to remind you that this tool supports *your action*. That means you have chosen this action because of a strong belief in its ability to impact your students' success and your success as an educator. Its purpose is to honor your ability to choose, to have your autonomy, and to celebrate your competence as an educator. Let me again clarify one thing, however: *autonomous* does not necessarily mean by yourself, unless you choose to define it that way. In fact, this plan will encourage you to engage with your colleagues whether you want your action plan to include a team goal or not. You are going to take the work you've done in the Reflection sections of this book and use it to complete the Autonomous Action Plan template. As you go through the template, you will focus on the needs of autonomy, competence, and relatedness. Your goal is to create an action plan that will start you on your way to continually expressing your unique talents and ideas—your voice—in your educational community.

Before you look at the Autonomous Action Plan template, let's revisit autonomy and competence.

Autonomy

In chapter 3 (page 35), I discussed the importance of autonomy as an innate need that, when fulfilled, allows you to feel empowered with a strong sense of well-being about your work. Although teacher autonomy seems to have come under attack in our current culture of public education, educators still have the ability to take autonomous action. Clearly, autonomy is not in the hands of those above you; it is in your hands. This need for autonomy also is not about ignoring larger obligations. You have responsibilities as a professional to fulfill the tasks and initiatives placed before you as an educator. However, you can do many things within the framework of these parameters to nurture autonomy and bring back a sense of ownership in your work. As a focused educator with much to offer, it is up to you to take action to implement what you feel will have an impact on the success of your students. This is your voice, your unique contribution, your action toward moving closer to your vision and purpose—your *why*. Autonomous action is part of this process because it is the vehicle to change. It's your freedom to experiment, implement, and ultimately change the systems that keep you in a victim mindset. So let's take a look at your autonomous actions. At the end of chapter 3 (page 44), I asked you to list those things that you had either researched or had determined from your own experience as an educator as capable of increasing your students' success rate if implemented. Revisit those now. You may have come up with just one or you may have several. It is possible that you have come up with more ideas since chapter 3. It doesn't matter how many ideas you found, just that you have an idea to implement that expresses your unique voice. I want you to list those ideas in your journal or on the lines below:

_____

_____

_____

_____

Some of you may have identified something personal, like a need for a plan to ensure better organization in your own classroom, or you may have a certain pedagogy you've wanted to implement, or a plan for more effective interventions, and still others may have an idea for more effective scheduling. The actions are as unique as you are, so there are no wrong or right choices as long as the ultimate goal is to increase student successes and achievement. These actions can be ones you take independently or ones you want to take collectively with your team. Let me also mention here that some of you may even have ideas you want to initiate with your principal or supervisor if it's a system-wide change you feel can make an impact. That's great! My only advice to you here is that if your principal or supervisor, after being shown the research and plan of action, is not open to the idea, you should go back to your list and choose again. Identify something on your list that can be implemented through your own actions, or through the actions of you and your team. Often, when you are successful in your individual classrooms or teams, you have the evidence and therefore more leverage when you want to grow the idea into a larger-scaled implementation. So don't be discouraged. Keep your vision clear and find a stepping stone that will lead you toward your ultimate goal.

Competence

In the discussion about competence, I describe how the ever-changing curriculums, programs, and reform initiatives can often make educators feel that they are not competent in anything. Teachers do what they are told to do, but they are not always sure that what they do will have the impact on student learning that is promised. When you reach a place in your educational practice where compliance outweighs innovation, again, you can be left feeling disengaged and unmotivated. You can feel incompetent. Of course, this is not true. You are very competent. When you are operating in a cloud of emotional overload, sometimes educators forget that they have many prized talents and gifts that they bring to their classrooms and colleagues that enhance student learning, and the efficacy of the school or department. Certainly, the list of autonomous actions you create is reflective of your success as an educator and your intuitive understandings about what students need to perform at high levels.

I discuss the SMART goal as a tool to help reinforce your competence and self-efficacy. Goal setting is a practice to ensure you recognize your successes and begin to understand clearly your competence as an educator. Teachers encourage students to build self-efficacy by setting goals, meeting those goals, and celebrating their successes—but educators themselves need to do this, too. You need to be clear about your goals so you can be clear about your successes and celebrate them with your students and colleagues. The act of filling out an action plan or creating a SMART goal does not inherently bring about feelings of competence; it is the passion behind the action you intend to take and your desire for its impact on student learning that create feelings of competence. Again, it is your voice and passion for results that drive your goals and actions. I want you to make goal setting a consistent practice in your work that elevates you to a higher level of engagement, success, and self-efficacy.

Having revisited some key areas, let's get started laying out a plan of action. As you go through the Autonomous Action Plan, focus on the following elements.

- Your knowledge as an educator
- Your autonomy to take action
- Your ability to engage and inspire others to join you in meeting your intended goal
- Your competence to meet that intended goal
- Your personal *why* and voice as an educator

Each section has examples to support you along the way. I hope that the end result will be a practice in goal setting that will resonate as authentic and empowering for you as an educator working to create positive change for yourself and your students.

Section One—The Action

Look at the first section of our Autonomous Action Plan: Section One—The Action. At the end of chapter 4 (page 64), I asked you to select just one of your actions and create a SMART goal to identify what your intended outcome would be after taking the action. Take a moment now and identify that action again, or if you feel that you would like to select another one at this time, do so. Once you have selected your action, fill out the first part of your template by answering the questions in Section One. In addition to writing your action and the steps you will take to achieve this action, identify research that supports this effort. If you're working with a team on this action, what common knowledge will you need? Write this down, too. If you came up with this action yourself but your team is working with you to accomplish it, your team will need to know the *why* of the action and be just as committed to the intended outcomes. Knowledge about the action helps ensure this.

An example of Section One completed by the Cottonwood Elementary School leadership team is shown in figure 6.1. Their goal is to create a more effective Response to Intervention (RTI) system of supports in their school through more strategic scheduling.

AUTONOMOUS ACTION PLAN

SECTION ONE—The Action
Beginning Date: 3/12

Action Statement: What is the action I (we) will take to address student learning needs based on current data?

The leadership team will audit the current practices for scheduling interventions and remediations. We want to ensure students who need extra time and support are receiving certain access to intervention and remediation, but are not being pulled out during essential learning being taught in the classroom. We will then create a schoolwide RTI schedule that ensures this through engaging teachers, support staff, special education (SPED) teachers, and remediation teachers in the process.

Steps:

- Utilize Pyramid Response to Intervention template to audit current RTI schedules and practices for supporting students who need extra academic and behavioral support.
- Identify students who are being pulled out of class for remediation during core instruction or intervention.
- If this is happening, look at the time frames in the current schoolwide schedule that are causing this to occur.
- Engage stakeholders working with students needing intervention or remediation to collaborate on a new schedule that prevents students from being pulled out during core grade-level instruction.
- Create a master schedule draft reflecting the proposed changes and ratify it with consensus feedback from teachers and stakeholders.

> **Rationale:** What does the research say about this action?
>
> "We have repeatedly stressed that interventions must be provided in addition to new essential grade-level curriculum, not in place of it. So when students fail to master essential standards—academic or behavioral—by the end of Tier 1, then the school must create a schedule in which these students can continue to work on this standard, while not missing new essential curriculum during core instruction." (p. 186)
>
> Buffum, A., Mattos, M., & Malone, J. (2018). *Taking action: A handbook for RTI at work*. Bloomington, IN: Solution Tree Press.
>
> **Collaborators:** If you are collaborating on this action, who is your team and what common knowledge will be necessary for you to work collaboratively?
>
> The leadership team will be working collaboratively with members of the SPED team, Title I support team, and ESL teachers. We will need to create collective knowledge about the differences between grade-level intervention and remediation practices and the need of students to have access to both if needed while not missing core instruction. We will also need to build consensus on how pull-outs that are not coordinated can actually create more gaps in learning for the student.

FIGURE 6.1: Autonomous Action Plan—Section One.

Section Two—The SMART Goal

Now look at Section Two—The SMART Goal. Again, you completed these steps at the end of chapter 4. If the goal you chose in chapter 4 is the same one you used to complete Section One on your template, go ahead and just plug in the SMART goal information from chapter 4 here. If you have decided on a different action, use the guidelines at the end of chapter 4 (page 64) to complete Section Two of your plan.

The example from the elementary school leadership team on their RTI goal is shown in figure 6.2 (page 108).

Section Three—My Posse

Your work on the SMART goal will guide you in examining the outcomes of the action you have decided to take. Now, complete Section Three of the Autonomous Action Plan. But before you move on, let's quickly revisit the topic of relatedness and talk about the importance of celebrations in your work to restore your internal culture.

AUTONOMOUS ACTION PLAN

SECTION TWO—SMART Goal
S—Who will this action impact and how?
Our students who are currently scoring below grade level on STAR Renaissance quarterly assessments will be impacted.
M—What positive change in learning data do you intend to accomplish?
We intend to increase the number of students scoring at grade level on the STAR assessment by 10 percent.
A—For how many students?
This would initially impact at least forty-six students grades K–5.
R—How will you know if your action has made an impact? What is your data point?
The number of students at or above grade level will increase by 10 percent on the STAR assessments.
T—When will you (your team) evaluate your impact? With what tool?
The leadership team will evaluate and compare data from the September beginning-of-the-year STAR assessments to the December mid-year STAR assessments and report to the school staff.
What is your SMART Goal?
By creating and implementing a coordinated schoolwide RTI schedule that eliminates pull-outs during core instruction, the number of students who score at grade level on the mid-year STAR assessments will increase from 37 percent (169 students) to 47 percent (215 students) on the mid-year STAR assessment given the week of December 5th.

FIGURE 6.2: Autonomous Action Plan—Section Two.

Relatedness

Remember that the research says that the innate need for relatedness is one of the most important human needs. Educators have so much on their plates and too often feel overwhelmed by it all. The PLC puts a focused emphasis on collaboration and collective commitments, which is not by chance. Extensive research shows a positive impact and results of collaborative teams in education (see DuFour et al., 2016, p. 77). You have an increased chance of successfully meeting the needs of every child when you bring in the varied and beautiful gifts and insights of a collaborative team of educators—their voices. So although at times you will take on goals and actions that are personal to you alone, it is still important that you tie this to the collective whole. Thus, I ask you to identify not only your team, if you are taking on this action with colleagues, but also your champions.

Champions are individuals in your school or department who honor your passion and drive to take on your chosen action and goal. These people will become your *posse* and support you while you support higher academic outcomes for students. They will be there when you begin the process, when you need to flesh something out in the middle, when you have setbacks that require rethinking the plan, and when you celebrate achieving your ultimate goal. We desperately need these champions and connections in our practices as educators. They represent relatedness at its best. This ability to share and relate to other educators will build and restore a climate and culture of relational trust in our schools and educational organizations. It's the most important component in this process because it ensures you're not alone and that you are fostering relatedness while you're on the journey.

Celebrations

The second part of this section asks you to define how you will celebrate both the actions you take and the results of those actions. In my experience, educators too often forget or neglect to celebrate themselves in the profession. Maybe it's because they think of celebrations as being more about the students (which is absolutely important and should probably be done even more frequently) but not really about how to celebrate themselves. That thinking must change. Celebrating your work and accomplishments is just as important for you as an educator as it is for your students. In this plan, you identify how you will celebrate yourself before you even begin. Make it part of the plan to ensure you don't neglect it when you actually accomplish your actions steps and then again when you reach your intended successes for your students. So, think really hard about this one. Think about what you and the educators who are supporting this action would want to do to celebrate your accomplishments. What would be fun? What would continue to reinforce and strengthen the bonds and relational trust you've created on this journey with your team, or with your champions? The celebrations will be as varied as the educators involved. So don't limit yourselves. Celebrate!

OK, now that you've revisited and clarified the importance of both relatedness and celebrations, go ahead and fill out Section Three of the Autonomous Action Plan. Another example from the leadership team plan is shown in figure 6.3 (page 110).

AUTONOMOUS ACTION PLAN

SECTION THREE—My Posse
Who will be your champion(s) as you pursue this goal? Our principal and assistant principal are part of the leadership team and are behind this goal 100 percent They are also going to share our plan with the Associate Superintendent who supervises our school. The Leadership Team members represent grades K–5, our counselor, instructional coach, and SPED teachers and Specials teachers. We intend to champion and support one another as we communicate and build consensus for this schoolwide adaptation to our master schedule to support RTI.
How will you celebrate this goal? After building consensus and implementing a new schedule: - Dinner at Marco's on the Water After increasing students' scoring at grade level or higher by 10 percent: - Schoolwide celebration and Crazy Hat Day - Associate Superintendent invited to staff meeting celebration to honor the teachers for their work

FIGURE 6.3: Autonomous Action Plan—Section Three.

Section Four—My Why, My Voice

This last section is all about empowerment. It's all about you, or you and your team. This section comes at the end of the plan so that you will be reminded why this plan matters. It's a place to reflect on that *why* statement you wrote down and the voice you plan to bring into the arena of education. This statement connects you with your passion and purpose. Whether your goal is big or small, a leap or a baby step, it's your contribution—it's your voice. This is an area just for you, or you and your team, to reflect on your purpose and the impact you intend to make in your career as an educator for the students you serve, and on how this action will bring you closer to your *why* and your purpose. If you are pursuing this goal with a team, this is also the place to clarify your collective purpose and vision as you work together to impact change (see figure 6.4, page 111).

AUTONOMOUS ACTION PLAN

SECTION FOUR—My *Why*, My Voice
How does this plan connect to your *why* as an educator? How does it highlight your voice?
As a leadership team at Cottonwood Elementary, our collective vision is to ensure high levels of learning for *all* of our students. Taking on the task of ensuring our master schedule is created in such a way that the needs of our most struggling students are not neglected or overlooked but instead prioritized is incredibly important to us. And it absolutely resonates with our collective purpose and passion as educators on the leadership team to work collaboratively to make the changes that ensure the success of our students, the teachers, and our school community as a whole.

FIGURE 6.4: Autonomous Action Plan—Section Four.

As you work on completing this Autonomous Action Plan for yourself or with your collaborative team, please remember that this is only a tool. Filling out an action plan alone does not create the empowerment that you are looking to nurture. Your belief in and intent to accomplish the action that you have chosen ensures your intention becomes a reality. This plan is unique because it's designed with the purpose of pulling together all the elements of autonomy, competence, and relatedness, and your *why* as an educator, in order to help you begin bringing that sense of happiness and well-being back into your profession.

Also, please consider that this is not a one-and-done activity. It is a commitment to the cycle of goal setting captured in the Plan, Do, Study, Act cycle of growth (Park, Hironaka, Carver, & Nordstrum, 2014). However, I'm asking you to consciously acknowledge the elements of autonomy, competence, relatedness, and your why each time you participate in action research. This is the focus that will inevitably begin to restore your internal culture; the cycle will begin to mitigate the victim mindset and replace it with a mindset of success and empowerment.

AUTONOMOUS ACTION PLAN

SECTION ONE—The Action
Beginning Date:

Action Statement: What is the action (we) will take to address student learning needs based on current data?

Steps:

-
-
-
-

Rationale: What does the research say about this action?

Collaborators: If you are collaborating on this action, who is your team and what common knowledge will be necessary for you to work collaboratively?

SECTION TWO—SMART Goal
S—Specific—Who will this action impact and how?
M—Measurable—What positive change in learning data do you intend to accomplish?
A—Attainable—For how many students?
R—Results Oriented—How will you know if your action has made an impact? What is your data point?
T—Time Bound—When will you (your team) evaluate your impact? With what tool?

What is your SMART Goal?

SECTION THREE—My Posse

Who will be your champion(s) as you pursue this goal?

How will you celebrate this goal?

SECTION FOUR—My *Why*, My Voice

How does this plan connect to your *why* as an educator? How does it highlight your voice?

Epilogue

As I began writing these last pages, the *Wall Street Journal* headlined an article titled, "Teachers Quit Jobs at Highest Rate on Record" (Hackman & Morath, 2018). This headline is indicative of how our media portray public education in our culture. News outlets rarely report good news about education, and often report bad news. The *Wall Street Journal* article focuses primarily on how low teacher pay contributes to the teacher exodus to increasing opportunities in job markets offering higher salaries than education. Yet, as educators, we know there is more to this migration than just money (although money is important). The twenty-eighth annual *MetLife Survey of the American Teacher* was completed in 2012 (MetLife, Inc., 2012). This comprehensive survey of school teachers and principals in the United States public education system reveals the following concerning statistics.

- Teachers' job satisfaction is down from 59 percent in 2009 to 44 percent in 2012, the smallest percentage stating satisfaction since 1989.
- Twenty-nine percent of teachers indicated they were likely to leave the profession within the next five years, up from 17 percent in 2009.
- High-poverty schools experienced a turnover rate roughly 50 percent higher than the rate in more affluent schools.
- Only 37 percent of principals and 27 percent of teachers in high-poverty schools said that students in their schools were performing at or above grade level.
- Fifty percent of principals and 51 percent of teachers felt under stress "several days a week" (MetLife, Inc., 2012).

In addition, the 2019 *Phi Delta Kappan* annual poll of attitudes about K–12 education reveals that 50 percent of public school teachers surveyed indicated they have thought of leaving the teaching profession completely. What should come as no surprise at this point is that 52 percent of those teachers indicated that the lack of voice and influence into the standards, testing, and curriculum initiated in their states, districts, and schools is one of the primary reasons for contemplating this exit (*Phi Delta Kappan*, 2019).

This is not a pretty picture by any means. Yet the following statistic from the 2012 MetLife survey may be the most disturbing.

- Forty-three percent of teachers were pessimistic that the level of student achievement would increase in the near future.

That's 43 percent! This statistic suggests that almost half of the teachers in public schools in the United States appear to have resigned themselves to the glaring achievement gaps that leave struggling students without the skills and resources to avoid or escape bleak circumstances that include unemployment, poverty, incarceration, and limited choices for improving their economic statuses.

The truth is that all of these statistics show the need to heal the internal culture of the educator. If teachers in American public schools had healthy internal cultures—positive internal perceptions and self-talk that support their beliefs about their capabilities to accomplish the task of ensuring all students learn at high levels—then we would never see statistics like the preceding ones. Unfortunately, the current culture of public education seems only to perpetuate this pessimism in its educators, primarily through the exclusion of educators from decision-making processes that would otherwise allow them the ability to innovate. The current systems in public education are set up to use educators as mechanisms for implementing programs and curriculums with educated children as the intended outcome—a ludicrous model comparable to the factory worker who is a mechanism for producing a car or other product. In a factory, a worker can just apply the right part at the right time and build a quality end product. Educating children does not work this way; children are not mass-produced, identical objects that come with a specific set of identical parts that fit into a one-size-fits-all program, curriculum, or assessment bank. Educating children requires the intuitive care of highly engaged teachers who use their talents as educators to meet the moral imperative of ensuring all students learn at high levels.

As I have said throughout this book, it is in your hands to turn the tide in public education, and work to create a culture that honors the educator. The continual practice of educators working collaboratively, setting goals, and working collectively to meet those goals through innovation and action research is what will turn this tide. You cannot be content to keep putting yourself in the role of implementer of teacher-proof programs. Programs, textbooks, computer-based technology—they have their place, but they never have and never will meet the needs of all students. They are not the silver bullets they are touted to be; *you* are the silver bullet. You are the one who will ultimately hit the target of learning for all.

I often tell the educators I work with that the answers to their challenges to meet the needs of all students lie within the school walls. It is not that you won't use the tools and researched practices developed in the field of education, but it's in your own intelligent, creative, and capable hands that they will have the intended impact. School reform will never be successful if educators do not embrace this truth; only when educators are free to utilize their knowledge and expertise in innovative and creative ways will we see students leaving our educational system with high academic skills, prepared to be the thought leaders and conscientious citizens our world so desperately needs.

So now the ball is in your court. Change must start with you—you and the educators you collaborate with each day. We have worked through activities and actions intended to help you tap into your deep sense of passion and purpose, to help you become more cognizant of your need for autonomy, competence, and relatedness to ensure a healthy internal culture and to once again find your unique voice as an educator. I have no doubt that you will tap into your courage and step into the arena of public education to make changes in your schools and organizations. And as you become part of these collective changes brought about by educators working together to solve the challenges that we face in public education, you will also begin to heal the internal culture of the educator—yours and those of your colleagues. I encourage you to continue to stay connected to your *why*, discover and nurture your voice, set goals that lead you to your greatness, and make connections with those in your organization whom you can take with you on this journey—together you will surely be the start of a movement that changes the culture of public education.

I am honored to be with you through the pages of this book. I look forward to hearing about your victories as you continue your work as an educational change maker. (Visit www.yourinternalculture.com to share your stories and offer feedback.) In closing, I leave you with a quote from Patanjali (Purushothaman, 2014) that has inspired my own growth toward empowerment in my profession as an educator. I hope it will inspire you, too, along the path.

> When you are inspired by some great purpose, some extraordinary project, all your thoughts break their bounds. Your mind transcends limitations, your consciousness expands in every direction, and you find yourself in a new, great and wonderful world. Dormant forces, faculties and talents become alive, and you discover yourself to be a greater person by far than you ever dreamed yourself to be. (p. 22)

References and Resources

Albright, M. (2010, June 15). Madeleine Albright: An exclusive interview. *Huffington Post*. Accessed at https://www.huffingtonpost.com/marianne-schnall/madeleine-albright-an- exc_b_604418.html on May 24, 2019.

Baard, P. P., Deci, E. L., & Ryan, R. M. (2004). Intrinsic need satisfaction: A motivational basis of performance and well-being in two work settings. *Journal of Applied Social Psychology*, 34(10), 2045–2068.

Bandura, A. (1994). Self-efficacy. In V.S. Ramachaudran (Ed.), *Encyclopedia of human behavior* (pp.71–81). New York: Academic Press.

Bandura, A. (1995). Preface. In A. Bandura (Ed.), *Self-efficacy in changing societies* (pp. ix-xiv). New York: Cambridge University Press.

Bryk, A., & Schneider, B. (2002). *Trust in schools: A core resource for improvement.* New York: Russell Sage Foundation.

Buffum, A., Mattos, M., & Malone, J. (2018). *Taking action: A handbook for RTI at work.* Bloomington, IN: Solution Tree Press.

Chatzky, J. (2013). *The difference: How anyone can prosper in even the toughest times.* New York: Random House.

Collins, J. (2001, October). Good to great. *Jim Collins*. Accessed at www.jimcollins.com/article_topics/articles/good-to-great.html on May 24, 2019.

Covey, S. R. (1989). *The 7 habits of highly effective people.* New York: Simon & Schuster.

Covey, S. R. (2004). *The 8th habit: From effectiveness to greatness.* New York: Free Press.

Cromwell, S. (2002). Is your school's culture toxic or positive? *Education World*. Accessed at www.educationworld.com/a_admin/admin/admin275.shtml on September 10, 2019.

Csikszentmihalyi, M. (1990). *Flow: The psychology of optimal experience*. New York: Harper & Row.

Csikszentmihalyi, M. (1997, July 1). Finding flow. *Psychology Today*. Accessed at www.psychologytoday.com/us/articles/199707/finding-flow on May 24, 2019.

Deci, E. L., Eghrari, H., Patrick, B. C., & Leone, D.R. (1994). Facilitating internalization: The self-determination theory perspective. *Journal of Personality, 62*(1), 119–142.

Deci, E. L. & Ryan, R. M. (2000). The "what" and "why" of goal pursuits: Human needs and the self-determination of behavior. Psychological Inquiry, 11(4), 227–268

Deci, E. L., & Ryan, R. M. (2008). Facilitating optimal motivation and psychological well-being across life's domains. *Canadian Psychology/Psychologie Canadienne, 49*(1), 14–23.

Doran, G. T. (1981). There's a S.M.A.R.T way to write management's goals and objectives. *Management Review, 70*(11), 35–36. Accessed at https://community.mis.temple.edu/mis0855002fall2015/files/2015/10/S.M.A.R.T-Way-Management-Review.pdf on May 24, 2019.

Drucker, P. (2008). *Management* (Rev. ed.). New York: HarperBusiness.

Duckworth, A. (2016). *Grit: The power of passion and perseverance*. New York: Scribner.

DuFour, R., DuFour, R., & Eaker, R. (2008). *Revisiting professional learning communities at work: New insights for improving schools*. Bloomington, IN: Solution Tree Press.

DuFour, R., DuFour, R., Eaker, R., Many, T. W., & Mattos, M. (2016). *Learning by doing: A handbook for professional learning communities at work* (3rd ed.). Bloomington, IN: Solution Tree Press.

DuFour, R., & Eaker, R. (1998). *Professional learning communities at work: Best practices for enhancing student achievement*. Bloomington, IN: Solution Tree Press.

Dweck, C. S. (2007). *Mindset: The new psychology of success*. New York: Ballantine Books.

Dynarski, M. (2016, December 8). Teacher observations have been a waste of time and money. *Brookings*. Accessed at www.brookings.edu/research/teacher-observations-have-been-a-waste-of-time-and-money on May 24, 2019.

Frankl, V. (1959; 2006). *A man's search for meaning.* Boston: Beacon Press.

Fullan, M. (2014). *The principal: Three keys to maximizing impact.* San Francisco: Jossey-Bass.

Hackman, M., & Morath, E. (2018, December 28). Teachers quit jobs at highest rate on record. *Wall Street Journal.* Accessed at www.wsj.com/articles/teachers-quit-jobs-at-highest-rate-on-record-11545993052 on May 24, 2019.

Hattie, J. (2009). *Visible learning: A synthesis of over 800 meta-analyses relating to achievement.* London: Routledge.

Kappel, M. (2017, November 3). 6 Strategies to resolve conflict at work. Accessed at www.entrepreneur.com/article/303617 on September 25, 2019.

Kappel, M. (2017, December 6). How to handle conflict at your business. *Forbes.* Accessed at www.forbes.com/sites/mikekappel/2017/12/06/how-to-handle-conflict-at-your-business/#5700328a75ad on September 19, 2019.

Kramer, S. V. (2015). *How to leverage PLCs for school improvement.* Bloomington, IN: Solution Tree Press.

Kramer, S. V. (2019, Summer). First thing: Why PLCs? *All Things PLC Magazine.* Bloomington, IN: Solution Tree Press.

Kramer, S. V., & Schuhl, S. (2017). *School improvement for all: A how-to guide for doing the right work.* Bloomington, IN: Solution Tree Press.

Locke, E. A., & Latham, G. P. (2006). New directions in goal-setting theory. *Current Directions in Psychological Science, 15*(5), 265–268.

Margolis, H., & McCabe, P. P. (2006). Improving self-efficacy and motivation: What to do, what to say. *Intervention in School and Clinic, 41*(4), 218–227.

Marzano, R. (2010). Teacher scales for reflective practice: Applying the "Art and Science of Teaching." Accessed at www.freeholdboro.k12.nj.us/cms/lib/NJ01001089/Centricity/Domain/320/MRL%20Teacher%20Scales%20Reflective%20Practice%20-%20Domain%201.pdf on September 12, 2019.

Merrow, J. (2017). *Addicted to reform: A 12-step program to rescue public education.* New York: The New Press.

MetLife, Inc. (2013, February). *MetLife survey of the American teacher: Challenges for school leadership.* Accessed at www.metlife.com/content/dam/microsites/about/corporate-profile/MetLife-Teacher-Survey-2012.pdf on May 24, 2019.

Morin, A. (2016, June 15). This is how your thoughts become your reality. *Forbes*. Accessed at www.forbes.com/sites/amymorin/2016/06/15/this-is-how-your-thoughts-become-your-reality/#3f061ee0528a on May 28, 2019.

Muhammad, A. (2015a). *Overcoming the achievement gap trap: Liberating mindsets to effect change*. Bloomington, IN: Solution Tree Press.

Muhammad, A. (2015b). *Victim mindset* [Video file]. Accessed at https://globalpd.com/search/content/MjY5 on May 28, 2019.

Muhammad, A. (2018). *Transforming school culture: How to overcome staff division* (2nd ed.). Bloomington, IN: Solution Tree Press.

Neck, C. P., & Manz, C. C. (1992). Thought self-leadership: The influence of self-talk and mental imagery on performance. *Journal of Organizational Behavior, 13*(7), 681–699.

O'Neill, J., & Conzemius, A. E. (2013). *The handbook for SMART school teams: Revitalizing best practices for collaboration*. Bloomington, IN: Solution Tree Press.

Park, S., Hironaka, S., Carver, P., & Nordstrum, L. (2014). *Continuous improvement in education*. Stanford, CA: Carnegie Foundation for the Advancement of Teaching. Accessed at www.carnegiefoundation.org/wp-content/uploads/2014/09/carnegie-foundation_continuous-improvement_2013.05.pdf on May 7, 2019.

Patanjali. (1975). *The Yoga sutras of Patanjali: The book of the spiritual man: An interpretation*. London: Walkins.

Patterson, K., Grenny, J., McMillan, R., Switzler, A. (2011). *Crucial conversations: Tools for talking when stakes are high* (2nd ed.). New York: McGraw-Hill.

Peale, N.V. (1952). *The power of positive thinking*. New York: Prentice-Hall.

Pennebaker, J. W. (1991). Writing your wrongs. *American Health, 10*, 64–67.

Pennebaker, J. W. (1997). *Opening up: The healing power of expressing emotions* (Rev. ed.). New York: Guilford Press.

Pennebaker, J. W. (2004). *Writing to heal: A guided journal for recovering from trauma & emotional upheaval*. Oakland, CA: New Harbinger Publications.

Pennebaker, J. W., & Smyth, J. (2016). *Opening up by writing it down: How expressive writing improves health and eases emotional pain* (3rd ed.). New York: Guilford.

Phi Delta Kappan. (2019). *PDK poll of the public's attitudes toward the public schools.* Accessed at https://pdkpoll.org/assets/downloads/2019pdkpoll51.pdf on August 26, 2019.

Pink, D. H. (2009). *Drive: The surprising truth about what motivates us.* New York: Riverhead Books.

Purushothaman, D. (2014). Words of wisdom (volume 46): 1001 Quotes & quotations. Kollam, Kerala, India: Centre for Human Perfection.

Riggs, L. (2013, October 18). Why do teachers quit? *The Atlantic.* Accessed at www.theatlantic.com/education/archive/2013/10/why-do-teachers-quit/280699 on May 28, 2019.

Ryan, R. M., & Deci, E. L. (2000). Self-determination theory and the facilitation of intrinsic motivation, social development, and well-being. *American Psychologist, 55*(1), 68–78.

Sinek, S. (2010). *How great leaders inspire action* [Video file]. Accessed at www.ted.com/talks/simon_sinek_how_great_leaders_inspire_action on May 28, 2019.

Sinek, S. (2011). *Start with why: How great leaders inspire everyone to take action.* New York: Portfolio/Penguin.

Sinek, S., Mead, D., & Docker, P. (2017). *Find your why: A practical guide for discovering purpose for you and your team.* New York: Portfolio.

Sparks, D. (2004). Broader purpose calls for higher understanding: An interview with Andy Hargreaves. *Journal of Staff Development, 25*(2), 46–50.

Taylor, S. E., & Pham, L. B. (1999). The effect of mental simulation on goal-directed performance. *Imagination, Cognition and Personality, 18*(4), 253–268.

Theory. (n.d.). *Center for Self-Determination Study.* Accessed at http://selfdetermination theory.org/theory on May 28, 2019.

United States Department of Education Office of the Secretary of Education. (2011, February 23). *Guidance on fiscal year 2010 School Improvement Grants under section 1003(g) of the Elementary and Secondary Education Act of 1965.* Accessed at https://files.eric.ed.gov/fulltext/ED565877.pdf on May 28, 2019.

Van den Broeck, A., Vansteenkiste, M., De Witt, H., Soenens, B., & Lens, W. (2010). Capturing autonomy, competence, and relatedness at work: Construction and the initial validation of the work-related basic need satisfaction scale. *Journal of Occupational and Organizational Psychology, 83*(4), 981–1002.

West, M. A. (2012). *Effective teamwork: Practical lessons from organizational research* (3rd ed.). West Sussex, UK: John Wiley & Sons.

Williams, K. (2014, August 5). *Smart goals drive the work of a collaborative team* [Video file]. Accessed at https://globalpd.com/search/content/MjE= on May 29, 2019.

Williams, K. C., & Hierck, T. (2015). *Starting a movement: Building culture from the inside out in professional learning communities.* Bloomington, IN: Solution Tree Press.

Zolli, A., & Healy, A. M. (2013). *Resilience: Why things bounce back.* New York: Simon & Schuster.

Index

A

acknowledging ideas and perspectives, 37–38
action research, 32, 36–51
action statements, 105–107
Addicted to Reform (Merrow), 13
American Recovery and Reinvestment Act of 2009, 2
autonomous action plans, 57, 59–60, 102–103, 105–106
    the action, 105–107
    autonomy, 103-104
    competency, 104-105
    my posse, 107–110
    my why, my voice, 110–111
    samples, 106–108, 111
    the SMART goal, 107
autonomy, 7–9, 32, 35–36, 103–104
    action research, 32, 36
    conditions supporting, 23–24, 27
    continuous improvement, 32
    defined, 24
    lack of, 13, 26–27, 35–36
    need for, 5–6
    reflecting on, 32–33
    reflection, 44
    supports for, 37–41
    tight and loose leadership, 32, 41–44
    vs. compliance, 35

B

Bandura, A., 14
building a framework, 29–32
burnout, 115–116

C

celebrations, 8, 32, 86
    autonomous action plan, 109
Center for Self-Determination Theory, 24
collaboration
    example, 28–29
    not valuing, 16
    PLC and, 30–32, 38, 42
collaborative teams
    collective competency and, 80–82
    resilience and, 76–87
    shared leadership and, 90–93
collective commitments
    example, 28–29
    PLC and, 30–31
collective competency, 80–82
collective responsibility, 42–43
    collaborative teams and, 82–83
    not valuing, 16
Collins, J., 78
Common Core Standards, 15
common ground, 85
communication norms, 83–85
compassion, 85
competence, 7–9, 30, 32, 45–46, 104–105
    celebrations, 32
    conditions supporting, 23–24
    defined, 25
    feeling of, 5–6
    focus on results, 32
    individual-level goal setting, 54–63
    predictable feedback, 28
    reflecting on, 32–33

reflection, 64
reflective practice through goal setting, 63–64
sense of incompetence, 46–50
setting goals for, 50
SMART goals, 32, 50–54
complacent teams, 75
compliance, 14–15
    vs. affecting change, 52–53
    vs. autonomy, 35
confidence
    eroding, 14–16
conflict, 83–85
    creating space for, 85
continuous improvement, 32
Covey, S., 98
creativity, 14, 23–24
critical/crucial conversation, 84
Csikzentmahalyi, M., 93
cultural change, 11
culture of public education, 7, 11
    defined, 12–13

D

Deci, E., 24, 35
despondency, 7, 43–44, 115–116
    transition to hope, 16–20
difficult life experiences, 9–10
divisive rhetoric, 12
Doran, G., 52
Drive (Pink), 36
driven teams, 75
Drucker, P., 52
DuFour, R., 76
Duncan, A., 2
dysfunctional teams, 74

E

Eaker, B., 76
Effective Teamwork (West), 71–72
The 8th Habit (Covey), 98
embracing conflict, 85

English-language learners, 1–3, 27
    example, 46–50
essential needs, 4–6
expectations
    high, 30
    low, 17, 21
    on educators, 72

F

fears, 100
feedback
    non-manipulative, 37–39
    predictable, 28
finding your voice, 8, 97–98
    autonomous action plans, 102–103
    letting go of the past, 101–102
    sharing it, 98–101
flow, 93–94
focus, 85–86
    on results, 6, 30–32
forgiveness, 85, 101–102
formative assessment, 42
fulfillment
    defining, 5–6
Fullan, M., 87

G

getting started, 10
goal setting, 8–10, 28, 104–105
    for competence and self-efficacy, 50
    individual level, 54–63
    reflection, 63–64
    SMART goals, 50–54
Good to Great (Collins), 78
grit, 14
growth mindset, 14
guiding coalition, 87–90

H

hardiness, 14
Hargreaves, A., 44

Hierck, T., 88
hopelessness. *See* despondency

I

incompetence
    recognizing and addressing, 46–50
initiative fatigue, 54–56, 115–116
internal culture of influence, 19–20
internal culture of the educator, 7, 11, 117–118
    culture of public education, 7, 11–13
    defined, 14–16
    internal culture of influence, 19–20
    reflection, 20–22
    school culture, 7, 12
    top-down culture of influence, 18
    transition from despondency to hope, 16–20
inter-team cooperation, 73
irresponsibility, 17, 21
isolation, 21, 25, 54–56
    vs. relatedness, 69–72

J

job satisfaction, 115–116
journaling, 9–10, 101–102

L

labeling, 4–6, 15
leadership
    shared, 32
    shared, 86–94
    tight and loose, 32, 41–44, 78
leadership team. *See* guiding coalition
Learning by Doing (DuFour et al.), 6, 41–42, 88
letting go of the past, 101–102
listening deeply, 85

M

Management Review, 52
Merrow, J., 13
MetLife Survey of the American Teacher, 115–116
mindsets, 7
    growth, 14
    victim, 17
    victim vs. empowerment, 100
motivation
    conditions supporting, 23–24
    low, 17, 21
Muhammad, A., 12, 17, 21
mutual respect, 83–85
my posse, 68
    autonomous action plan, 107–110

N

No Child Left Behind (NCLB), 2, 16–17
    effects on teacher autonomy, 36

O

opportunities for choice, 37, 39–40
optimism, 14
organizing priorities, 9–10

P

pacing guides, 47
path forward, 7–9
Pennebaker, J., 9–10, 101–102
persistence, 23–24
Peterson, K., 12
Phi Delta Kappan, 115–116
Pink, D., 36
Plan, Do, Study, Act (Park et al.), 111
Professional Learning Communities at Work (PLC) process, 6–7, 20, 26, 46
    action research, 32, 36–41
    collaboration, 30–31
    collective commitments, 30–31
    example of, 27–29
    focus on results, 30–32
    framework for growth, 29–32
    resilience and the collaborative team, 76–87
    shared leadership and, 86–93
    supports of, 32

three big ideas of, 30
tight and loose leadership, 32, 41–44
poverty, 115
powerlessness, 21, 97–98
countering, 4–6
The Principal (Fullan), 87
Professional Learning Communities at Work (DuFour & Eaker), 76
providing meaningful information, 37–39
purpose, 78–80
pyramid response, 106

R

Race to the Top (RTTT), 16–17, 106
effects on teacher autonomy, 36
reflections
autonomy, 44
goal setting, 63–64
importance of, 9–10
internal culture of the educator, 20–22
relatedness, 94–95
Self–Determination Theory, 32–33
SMART goals, 64–66
Reflective writing. *See* journaling; reflections
relatedness, 7–9, 32, 67
autonomous action plans, 108–109
collaboration, 32
conditions supporting, 23–24
defined, 25, 69–72
example, 28–29
five indicators of team effectiveness, 72–76
need for, 5–6
PLC and, 30–31
reflecting on, 32–33
reflection, 94
relational trust, 32
resilience and the collaborative team, 76–86
shared leadership, 32, 86–94
trust, 16, 32, 38, 81
what it offers, 67–69

relational trust, 16, 32, 38, 81
resentments, 10
resilience, 14
resilient teams, 75–76
revising your why, 33–34
Revisiting Professional Learning Communities at Work (DuFour et al.), 88
Ryan, R., 24, 35

S

scaffolding, 47–48
school culture, 7
defined, 12
School Improvement Grant (SIG) money, 2
Self-Determination Theory (SDT; Ryan & Deci), 5–7, 23
building a framework, 29–32
collaborative culture, 30–31
defined, 24–29
focus on learning, 30
focus on results, 30–31
reflection, 32–33
revisiting your why, 33–34
three big ideas of PLC, 30
self-efficacy, 15
competence, 44–50
defined, 14
setting goals for, 50–63
self-initiation
encouraging, 37, 40–41
self-talk, 18–19
The 7 Habits of Highly Effective People (Covey), 98
shared leadership, 32, 86–87
collaborative teams and, 90–93
finding your flow, 93–94
guiding coalition, 87–90
shutting down, 69–72
silo effect, 90
Sinek, S., 33–34
SMART goals, 32, 50–53, 104–108
collaborative teams and, 77, 80–82

defined, 52–54
reflection, 64–66
Social reflexivity, 73, 79
    average, 75
    high, 75–76
    low, 74
Start With Why (Sinek), 33–34
Starting a Movement (Williams & Hierck), 80, 88
supports for autonomy, 37
    acknowledging ideas and perspectives, 37–38
    encouraging self-initiation, 37, 40–41
    providing meaningful information, 37–39
    providing opportunities for choice, 37, 39–40

T

Take Action (Buffum et al.), 107
task reflexivity, 73–74
    average, 75
    high, 75–76
    low, 74
task-related objectives, 72
teacher accountability, 15–16
teacher evaluations, 4
Teacher Scales for Reflective Practice (Marzano), 57–58
teacher-proofing schools, 13, 36
team effectiveness
    indicators of, 72–75
    resilience and, 76–87
team innovation, 73
team member well-being, 72
team viability, 72
tight and loose leadership, 32, 41–44
tools for success, 9–10
top-down culture of influence, 18
    mandates, 31–32, 36
toxic norms, 12
transformational model, 2

Transforming School Culture (Muhammad), 12
turnaround model, 2–3, 6, 8–9
    example, 25–29

U

U.S. Department of Education, 2
unchallenged belief systems, 12
unwavering belief in educators, 12–13

V

victim mindset, 17
    vs. empowerment, 100

W

Wall Street Journal, 115
West, M., 71–73, 79, 90, 94
why statements, 33–34, 103–104, 99
    autonomous action plan, 110–111
    sample, 34
Williams, K., 80, 88

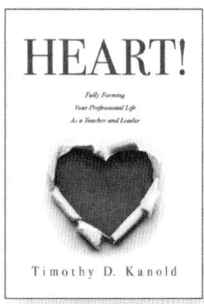

HEART!
Timothy D. Kanold

Explore the concept of a heartprint—the distinctive impression an educator's heart leaves on students and colleagues during his or her professional career. Use this resource to reflect on your professional journey and discover how to increase efficacy, and foster productive, heart-centered classrooms and schools.
BKF749

180 Days of Self-Care for Busy Educators
Tina H. Boogren

Rely on 180 Days of Self-Care for Busy Educators to help you lead a happier, healthier more fulfilled life inside and outside of the classroom. With Tina H. Boogren's guidance, you will work through 36 weeks of self-care strategies during the school year.
BKF920

Take Time for You
Tina H. Boogren

The key to thriving as a human and an educator rests in self-care. With Take Time for You, you'll discover a clear path to well-being. The author offers manageable strategies, reflection questions, and surveys that will guide you in developing an individualized self-care plan.
BKF813

The Beginning Teacher's Field Guide:
Tina H. Boogren

The joys and pains of starting a teaching career often go undiscussed. This guide explores the personal side of teaching, offering crucial advice and support. The author details six phases every new teacher goes through and outlines classroom strategies and self-care practices.
BKF806

Visit SolutionTree.com or call 800.733.6786 to order.

Wait! Your professional development journey doesn't have to end with the last pages of this book.

We realize improving student learning doesn't happen overnight. And your school or district shouldn't be left to puzzle out all the details of this process alone.

No matter where you are on the journey, we're committed to helping you get to the next stage.

Take advantage of everything from **custom workshops** to **keynote presentations** and **interactive web and video conferencing**. We can even help you develop an action plan tailored to fit your specific needs.

Let's get the conversation started.

Call 888.763.9045 today.

solution-tree.com